SAUTÉS

David DiResta and Joanne Foran

BRISTOL PUBLISHING ENTERPRISES
San Leandro, California

A Nitty Gritty® Cookbook

ISBN 1-55867-139-0

Cover design: Frank J. Paredes
Cover photography: John A. Benson
Food stylist: Suzanne Carreiro
Illustrator: James Balkovek

CONTENTS

ABOUT SAUTÉING

Sauté cooking is the choice of busy cooks who wish to serve delicious foods, cooked in a healthy manner and in a very short amount of time. Chicken, meats and seafoods are browned and succulent, vegetables are tender-crisp and colorful, and cleanup is minimal.

SAUTÉING DEFINED

The basic principles for sautéing (nearly indistinguishable from stir-frying) are simply searing in the natural flavors and juices of foods in a very small amount of fat, keeping the foods in motion and often reducing the heat settings from hot to medium.

Sautéing begins with a hot skillet. But depending on the thickness and materials of the skillet and the type of stovetop heating element, you may need to cook over a medium-high or high heat setting. Next, a small amount of fat is added to the skillet. Follow the recommended amounts in each recipe, but in many recipes we like to combine equal amounts of butter and oil for a desirable flavor. As soon as the oil is hot and butter is bubbly, add your foods. Brown and sear all the sides of the food to lock in the flavor. The browned particles of food that stick to the bottom of the skillet will be used for sauces and gravies.

TOOLS OF THE TRADE: COOKWARE

Good cooking begins with tested recipes and quality cooking tools. When purchasing new cookware, you want to look for durability, heat conductivity, comfort and a long-term warranty.

There are a large number of cookware manufacturers and many combinations of materials to choose from with a huge range of quality, from poor to excellent.

Key Features of Superior Cookware

- even heat distribution
- solid, sturdy construction
- heavy-gauge materials
- riveted handles
- oven-safe and broiler-safe pans and handles
- nonporous surface to prevent food from interacting with cookware
- easy to clean and resistant to scratches
- long-term warranty (minimum 10 years)
- customer service hot-line to answer your questions

SIZES AND SHAPES

Most manufacturers offer a large range of skillets from 7 inches to 14 inches across. The sides are sloped and the depth is $1\frac{1}{2}$ to $2\frac{1}{2}$ inches. This classic design is the traditional shape of an omelet pan, and you may find that many brands label this shape as their omelet skillet and the straight-sided pan as their sauté pan. However, the slope-sided skillet is the most popular shape for preparing sautés. The contoured sides are ideal for sautéing and allow for easy use of a spatula for turning, stirring, flipping and removing foods.

Since you don't want to overcrowd your food or allow excess room in the skillet, it's important to have a variety of sizes on hand to accommodate varying quantities of ingredients. The 8-, 10- and 12-inch skillets are the most popular sizes and will adapt to recipes from 2 to 6 servings.

slope-sided skillet, fry pan or omelet pan
The most versatile sauté pan, ideal for sautéing meats, vegetables, seafood and fruits. 7-14 inches

straight-sided sauté pan
The deep straight sides increase the pan's capacity, allowing browning, covering and simmering. Good for large quantities of stews and sautés. 1 - 7 quarts

fajita pan
For preparing and presenting sautéed meats and vegetables for Mexican fare.

stir-fry pan
For quick, easy and nutritious Oriental-style cuisine.

COVERS

Since most sauté recipes begin with searing foods at a high or medium-high temperature followed by reducing the heat setting, you should have covers for your skillets. Covers should be well constructed and should fit the skillets securely. Solid metal covers are perfectly adequate, but you may consider purchasing lids made from clear tempered glass, reinforced with a solid rim. A glass lid allows you the convenience of checking your foods without disturbing the cooking process. Covers should fit well and fairly securely. Both solid metal and glass tempered covers with reinforced rims are good choices.

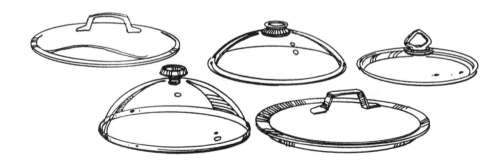

HANDLES

Handles play an integral part in the design and performance of your cookware. Solid metal handles are extremely durable and allow you to place the entire pan in the oven or under the broiler at high temperatures, which is necessary for some recipes. However, these handles will get hot setting over a stovetop burner for an extended length of time, so you'll need a pot holder or mitt to hold the skillet. Fortunately, many cookware companies offer stay-cool handle covers that fit snugly over the metal handles for stovetop use. Before you purchase your cookware, hold the skillet in your hand and judge the comfort. Be sure the handles are securely attached to the skillet. Riveted handles last longer than spot-welded handles. Permanently molded stay-cool handles made from heat-resistant plastic or *phenolicresin* are usually comfortable and less industrial-looking, but they are not broiler-safe or as durable as the solid metal handles.

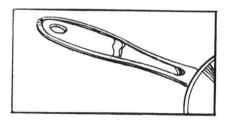 

What About Nonstick Cookware?

We were first introduced to nonstick cookware in the 1960s when Teflon-coated pans made a huge splash on the market. Unfortunately, these early coatings were soft and had a relatively short life. Today many brands of nonstick cookware utilize modern technology to attach the nonstick surface to cookware almost permanently, thereby allowing a cook to use metal utensils. But even if a quality nonstick material is applied, it must be attached to a well-designed skillet constructed with good materials.

Foods cooked in a nonstick skillet will release effortlessly, and cleanup will simply require a sponge and mild detergent. Although you don't need oil or butter to prevent sticking, you'll find that cooked foods will be rubbery and less flavorful if sautéed in a completely dry skillet. It is often difficult, and sometimes impossible, to sear foods and create the most desirable texture in a nonstick skillet. But for the health-conscious cook and for preparing certain foods, including pancakes, grilled vegetables and delicate toppings, we recommend adding a couple of nonstick skillets to your collection of cookware. Judge the quality of the skillet just as you would any other cookware and be sure to use the proper utensils and follow the recommended cooking, use and cleaning instructions so you don't void the warranty.

COOKWARE MATERIALS

The important qualities in cookware are heat distribution, conductivity and durability.

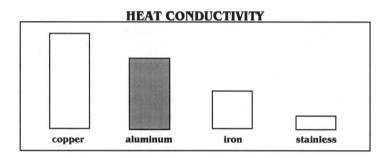

HEAT CONDUCTIVITY

copper   aluminum   iron   stainless

Copper

Copper is the most efficient and temperature-sensitive material for conducting heat in cookware. But you should not cook on a copper surface, because copper can leach into your foods and cause sickness. Quality copper cookware is the choice of many professional chefs, but it's also quite expensive. Traditional copper cookware has a relatively short life because the interior tin lining wears off, and it can be very difficult to locate a craftsperson to retin the cookware. Fortunately, there are many beautiful brands of exceptionally high-quality copper cookware that are permanently lined with stainless steel or nickel. Such pans are widely available in better department stores, gourmet kitchenware shops and by mail order.

Aluminum

Slightly less heat-sensitive than copper and 10 times more conductive than stainless steel is aluminum, a top choice for cookware by many of today's professional chefs and home cooks. Look for hard-anodized aluminum cookware. It's reasonably priced and offers all the qualities a cook needs in fine cookware. An electrochemical process actually changes the structure of the aluminum and creates a hard, stick-resistant, nonreactive pan that's perfect for sautéing. The pans are durable and nonporous and will never react chemically to sauces or other sensitive recipes. Professional heavy gauge hard-anodized is recommended and is ideally suited for home kitchens. The pans will heat up quickly and evenly over medium heat and retain their temperature. The hard surface is stick-resistant and allows you to use metal utensils. These pans are easy to care for and should be thoroughly cleaned after each use. Do not allow any residue to build up on the surface. If used properly, a well-manufactured anodized pan should last a lifetime.

Iron

These classicly shaped pans made of iron or rolled steel have been in use for many years. They heat up quickly, conduct heat reasonably well and have excellent heat retention. They are inexpensive and extremely durable. Unfortunately they rust easily and need to be carefully dried out and oiled after each use. Compared to the modern technologies applied to cookware, these are conveniences and advantages you'll sacrifice if you limit your cookware collection to these pans. Given their low cost and traditional value, they're a great option for a price-sensitive consumer.

Enamel on Metal

To prevent rusting and sticking, several manufacturers produce iron and steel pans with an attractive porcelain enamel finish on the interior and exterior of the pans. The enamel is often sheathed in several layers and comes in a wide range of attractive colors. The porcelain is nonporous and very easy to clean. The quality of porcelain enamel ranges from poor to excellent. To prevent chipping, the rims of the pans should be protected with a solid metal, preferably stainless steel, and the gauge of the steel should be moderately heavy. Look for good solid construction with riveted handles from a reputable company.

Stainless

Although solid stainless steel pans are easy to clean and very durable, they are not a good conductor of heat. But there are many high-quality brands of stainless steel cookware that offer superior conductivity and heat distribution. Through a process of tri-ply construction a thick layer of aluminum is sandwiched between two layers of quality stainless steel, or a layer of aluminum is bonded with an interior of stainless steel and an exterior of dark anodized aluminum. The aluminum core runs across the entire bottom of the pans, and some brands actually allow the aluminum to run up the sides.

These pans combine the beauty of stainless steel with the preferred heating properties of aluminum. These durable and functional pans are usually dishwasher-safe, oven- and broiler-proof, and allow you to use metal utensils. They are not stick-free or stick-resistant and require the use of oil or butter to prevent sticking. These quality stainless steel pans are a good option and are strongly recommended. But not all stainless steel tri-ply cookware pans are equal in quality or function, so before you purchase your cookware, check the manufacturer's warranty, the weight and the construction of the pan, including the handle.

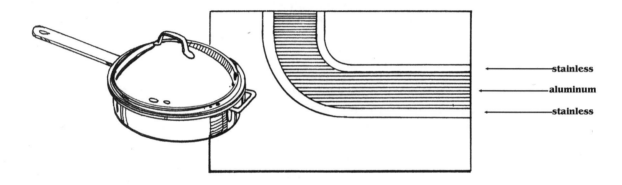

stainless
aluminum
stainless

FISH SAUTÉS

SAUTÉED FRESH FISH FILLETS
WITH SMOOTH APRICOT SAUCE

For sautéing fillets of semi-firm fresh fish, such as haddock, cod, halibut, grouper or snapper, have your fish monger leave the skin on one side of the fish. The skin prevents the fish from falling apart when you flip or remove it from the skillet. Or coat the fish with skim milk and dredge in flour, breadcrumbs, cornmeal or a combination for protection. For best results, always cook fish for 10 minutes per inch. This dish goes nicely with a baked potato and a fresh garden salad.

2 tsp. cornstarch
2 tbs. apricot brandy
¼ cup apricot preserves
1 clove garlic, minced or pressed
1 lb. fresh fish fillets
2 tbs. breadcrumbs
2 tbs. cornmeal
¼ cup milk
4 tsp. butter
4 tsp. olive oil
fresh cilantro or parsley sprigs for garnish

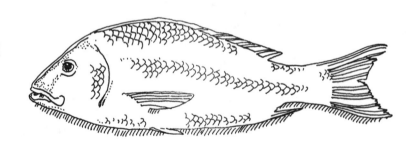

In a small bowl, whisk together cornstarch and brandy. In a small saucepan, combine apricot preserves, cornstarch-brandy mixture and garlic. Heat over medium-low heat until sauce just thickens. Stir thoroughly, and keep warm over very low heat. Rinse fish and pat dry. In a shallow bowl, mix together breadcrumbs and cornmeal. Pour milk into another shallow bowl and coat all sides of fish with milk. Dredge fish in breadcrumb mixture. Melt butter in a skillet. Add oil and heat over medium-high heat. If fish has skin, cook skinless side first. Sauté fish for 2½ minutes on each side. Place cooked fish on warm individual serving plates. Cover fish with equal portions of apricot sauce. Garnish with cilantro or parsley sprigs.

SWORDFISH WITH GARLIC AND FETA

Servings: 4

We prefer to sauté this recipe in a skillet with a smooth finish, such as stainless steel, anodized aluminum or a nonstick finish that can withstand a high heat setting.

2 lb. swordfish, tuna, marlin or halibut
  steaks
2 tbs. olive or canola oil
3 tbs. unsalted butter
1/4 cup fresh lemon juice
1/4 cup fresh lime juice

2 cloves garlic, minced or pressed
1 tsp. dried dill weed
1/2 cup crumbled feta cheese (can be
  reduced fat)
fresh parsley or cilantro sprigs for garnish

Rinse fish and pat dry. Divide fish into 4 equal pieces. Heat oil and 2 tbs. of the butter in a 10- to 14-inch skillet over medium-high heat. Cook fish for 4 to 7 minutes on each side, depending on thickness of fish. Use a sharp knife to test fish. It is done when the flesh of the thickest part is opaque. Transfer fish to ovenproof plates and place in a preheated 200° oven to keep warm. Add remaining 1 tbs. butter, lemon and lime juices, garlic and dill to remaining liquid in skillet. Heat over medium-low heat for 2 minutes or until garlic is lightly browned. Use a spatula to scrape browned bits from skillet to flavor sauce. Spoon sauce over cooked fish. Sprinkle with crumbled feta cheese. Garnish with fresh herb sprigs. Serve immediately.

PAN-FRIED SWORDFISH WITH CUCUMBER SALSA

Servings: 2

Here's a refreshing seafood dish for a hot summer day. You can substitute any pan-fried fish for the swordfish. Just remember the rule for cooking fish: 10 minutes of cooking time for every inch of thickness.

2 swordfish steaks, 8 oz. each
1 tbs. olive or canola oil
1 tsp. butter
½ cup diced cucumber
1 cup diced tomato

¼ cup finely chopped red onion
1 tbs. fresh lime juice
1 tsp. grated fresh lime rind (zest)
2 tsp. chopped fresh cilantro

Rinse fish and pat dry. Heat oil and butter in a skillet over medium heat. Place fish in skillet and sauté for 4 minutes. Turn fish over and cook for 4 more minutes or until fish is opaque. While fish is cooking, combine all remaining ingredients in a bowl. Transfer cooked fish to individual serving plates and top with tomato-cucumber salsa.

BLACKENED FISH FILLETS

You'll need a skillet that can withstand a very high temperature, such as a heavy cast iron or hard anodized aluminum to produce this Louisiana-style recipe. The intense heat may cause permanent damage to tri-ply or cookware with a nonstick coating. Fortunately most major cookware companies offer a toll-free consumer hot line to answer these questions.

1 lb. fish fillets — salmon, tuna, swordfish, red snapper or shad
1/4 cup melted butter, olive oil or canola oil
1/3 cup *Blackening Spice Mixture*, follows
2 tsp. *Herb Butter*, follows
4 lemon wedges
fresh parsley or cilantro sprigs for garnish

Rinse fish and pat dry. Brush fish with melted butter or oil. Pour *Blackening Spice Mixture* onto a sheet of waxed paper or into a shallow bowl. Dredge fish in mixture, covering both sides. Heat a heavy skillet to a very hot temperature over high heat. Cook fish for 2 to 3 minutes on each side or until center of fish is opaque and separates easily with a fork. Top fish with a dollop of *Herb Butter*. Transfer to individual serving plates. Serve with lemon wedges. Garnish with a sprig of parsley or cilantro.

BLACKENING SPICE MIXTURE

Yield: about 1/3 cup

1 tbs. paprika
1 tbs. onion powder
1 tbs. garlic powder
1 tbs. black pepper
2 tsp. dried thyme

1 tsp. dried oregano
1/2 tsp. cayenne pepper
1 tsp. chili powder
1/4 tsp. salt

Combine all ingredients in a small bowl and store in an airtight container. Keep in a dark area, such as a drawer or kitchen cabinet, and use sparingly.

HERB BUTTER

Yield: 1/2 cup

Flavored butters are easy to make and add zip to your meals. Try this on cooked foods or use for sautéing. The horseradish flavor is especially good on cooked fish.

1/2 cup butter, softened
juice of 1/2 lemon

1/2 tsp. dried basil
1 clove garlic, minced or pressed

Cream butter. Combine all ingredients in a food processor or blend together in a small bowl with a fork or spoon. Keep refrigerated or freeze for future use. Serve over poultry, fish, lamb or vegetables.

VARIATION: HORSERADISH BUTTER

Replace garlic and basil with 1 tbs. freshly grated horseradish.

SEARED TUNA WITH PEPPERY ONIONS

Servings: 2

Searing the fish allows it to cook in its natural juices. Fresh swordfish also works nicely in this recipe. The balsamic vinegar adds a celebrated flavor to this popular dish. Good with rice and sautéed squash.

2 tbs. canola or olive oil
1 cup chopped sweet onion — Vidalia, Granex, Grano or Walla Walla
1 can (4.5 oz.) chopped green chile peppers, drained, or ¼ cup fresh
¼ cup balsamic vinegar
¼ tsp. pepper

⅛ tsp. dried basil
1 lb. tuna steaks, about 8 oz. each
¼ cup flour
¼ tsp. dried thyme
⅛ tsp. rubbed sage
¼ cup skim milk

Heat 1 tbs. of the oil in a nonstick skillet. Add onion and sauté over medium-high heat for 4 to 5 minutes or until soft and golden brown. Add chopped peppers, vinegar, pepper and basil. Cook for 2 more minutes, stirring constantly. Remove from skillet and set aside. Rinse fish and pat dry. In a shallow bowl, combine flour, thyme and sage. Dip fish in milk and dredge in flour mixture. Heat remaining 1 tbs. oil in same skillet over medium-high heat. Sauté tuna for 3 to 4 minutes on each side or until fish is just cooked through. Transfer fish to warm serving plates over sautéed onions. Serve immediately.

SAUTÉED SOLE WITH PECAN COATS

You can replace the sole with any of the flounder fish. For a nice combination, serve this dish with mashed potatoes and a crisp salad. For easy cleanup and cooking, cook it in a nonstick or stick-resistant skillet.

1/4 cup pecans, finely chopped
1/4 tsp. garlic powder
1/4 tsp. paprika
1/4 tsp. onion powder
1/4 tsp. red pepper flakes
1/4 tsp. pepper
1/4 tsp. dried thyme
1/4 tsp. dried oregano

1/4 cup flour
1 lb. sole fillets
1/2 cup skim milk
2 tbs. olive or canola oil
1 tsp. chopped fresh parsley
6 lemon wedges
fresh mint sprigs for garnish

Place pecans in a dry nonstick skillet over medium heat and stir constantly until lightly toasted. In a shallow bowl, combine garlic powder, paprika, onion powder, red pepper flakes, pepper, thyme, oregano, flour and pecans. Rinse fish and pat dry. Dip fish in milk and dredge in flour-pecan mixture. Heat oil in a large nonstick skillet over medium-high heat. Sauté fish for 2 minutes on each side or until just cooked through. Transfer fish to serving plates. Sprinkle with fresh parsley and serve with lemon wedges. Garnish with sprigs of mint.

RED SNAPPER WITH
SWEET BALSAMIC SAUCE

Somewhere between a clove of garlic and a common onion lies the distinctive size and flavor of the shallot. Look for shallots in your supermarket along with other members of the onion family, including garlic and leeks. Sautéed shallots take on a mellow flavor and lend aroma to other foods. Give them a try.

1½ lb. red snapper, about 3 fillets
⅓ cup flour
¼ tsp. salt
¼ tsp. pepper
¼ tsp. dried basil
1 tbs. butter
1 tbs. olive oil

¼ cup minced shallots
½ cup white wine
⅔ cup chicken broth
1 tbs. chopped fresh cilantro
3 tbs. balsamic vinegar
1 tbs. brown sugar
fresh cilantro sprigs for garnish

Rinse fish and pat dry. In a shallow bowl, combine flour, salt, pepper and basil. Dredge fish in flour mixture. Melt butter with oil in a skillet over medium-high heat. As butter comes to a bubbling point, add fish and sauté on each side for 2 to 4 minutes or until just cooked through. Remove fish from skillet and place on 2 warm individual serving plates. Keep fish warm in a preheated 140° oven. Add shallots to skillet and sauté over medium heat for 2 minutes. Add wine, chicken broth and chopped cilantro;

cook for 5 minutes. Add vinegar and brown sugar. Stir frequently and cook for 5 minutes over a low heat. Scrape cooked browned bits from skillet while stirring. Pour sauce over fish. Serve immediately, garnished with fresh sprigs of cilantro.

VARIATION: FRESH HERB SAUCE

Yield: about 1 cup

Serve over sautéed fish, chicken or vegetables, or fresh pasta. Also delicious when dried herbs are substituted — just use 1/3 the quantities called for.

1 tbs. butter
1 tbs. cornstarch
1 cup chicken broth
1 tbs. chopped fresh basil
1 tbs. chopped fresh parsley

1/2 tbs. chopped fresh tarragon
1/8 tsp. salt
1/8 tsp. pepper
1 tsp. fresh lemon juice
1/2 tsp. fresh lime juice

Melt butter in an 8- to 10-inch skillet over medium heat. Add cornstarch and stir continuously for 1 minute. Add 1/2 cup of the chicken broth and stir continuously until mixture is well blended. Add remaining chicken broth, basil, parsley, tarragon, salt and pepper. Bring to a quick boil. Reduce heat to low and simmer uncovered for 20 minutes, stirring frequently. Add lemon and lime juices and mix thoroughly.

SAUTÉED SHARK WITH FENNEL AND CURRY

Servings: 2

If you can't find ground fennel, simply grind fennel seed with a mortar and pestle or spice grinder. Swordfish and tuna have a firm texture similar to shark and can be used as a substitution.

1 lb. shark
1/4 cup fresh lemon juice
1/4 tsp. ground fennel seeds

1/4 tsp. curry powder
2 tbs. olive or canola oil
fresh cilantro or basil leaves for garnish

Rinse fish and pat dry. In a shallow bowl, combine lemon juice, fennel, curry and 1 tbs. of the oil. Add fish, coating all sides; cover and marinate in the refrigerator for 2 hours. Heat remaining 1 tbs. oil in a skillet over medium heat. Add fish and sauté for 4 to 5 minutes on each side. Reserve remaining marinade. Place cooked fish on warm individual serving plates. Pour remaining marinade in skillet. Heat for 2 to 3 minutes. Scrape cooked bits from skillet into sauce. Cover fish with equal portions of lemon sauce. Garnish with cilantro or basil leaves. Serve at once.

VARIATION

Substitute fresh lime juice for the lemon juice or top fish with a 1/4 cup fresh salsa.

FRESH SALMON WITH CITRUS AND SHERRY

In this recipe you may substitute other semi-firm fresh fish steaks, including cod, snapper, halibut, pike or hake. This dish goes well with cooked asparagus spears.

2 salmon steaks, 6-8 oz. each
1 cup water
3/4 cup sherry
1 tbs. fresh lemon juice
1 tsp. fresh lime juice
1/4 tsp. pepper
1/4 tsp. paprika
1/2 tsp. dry mustard

1/2 tsp. dried thyme
1/8 tsp. garlic powder
1/4 tsp. dried marjoram
1 cup minced yellow onion
2 tsp. butter
2 tsp. cornstarch
fresh cilantro sprigs for garnish
4-6 lemon wedges for garnish

Rinse fish and pat dry. Pour water, sherry and juices into a straight-sided sauté pan. Bring to a boil. Stir in pepper, paprika, mustard, thyme, garlic powder and marjoram. Partially cover; reduce heat and simmer for 10 minutes. Distribute onion evenly on bottom of pan. Place fish on top of onion. Do not overlap fish. Cover pan and cook for 10 minutes over medium heat. Use a slotted spatula and slotted spoon to transfer onion and fish from skillet to warm serving plates. Melt butter in skillet, add cornstarch and stir constantly until sauce thickens, scraping cooked bits from pan into sauce. Pour over fish and serve immediately. Garnish with cilantro and lemon wedges.

SAUTÉED SALMON WITH TOASTED ALMOND CRUST

You'll appreciate the nutty flavor and crusty texture the almond topping adds. To prevent the fish from falling apart, leave the skin on one side and cook the skinless side first. This fish goes well with a perfectly baked potato and steamed broccoli.

2 tbs. sliced almonds
1/4 cup flour
1/4 tsp. dried basil
1/8 tsp. salt
1/4 tsp. pepper

2 salmon steaks, 6-8 oz. each
1 tbs. plus 2 tsp. canola or olive oil
1 tbs. butter
4-6 fresh lemon wedges
fresh cilantro or basil leaves for garnish

Place almond slices in a dry nonstick skillet over medium-low heat. Stir frequently for 2 to 3 minutes or until bright golden brown. Let almonds cool. Pound with a mallet or grind with a mortar and pestle or a small food processor until nuts are fine and semi-powdery. In a shallow bowl, combine almond powder, flour, basil, salt and pepper. Rinse fish and pat dry. Liberally coat all sides of salmon with 2 tsp. of the oil. Dredge salmon in almond mixture. Melt butter with 1 tbs. of the oil in a nonstick skillet over medium-high heat. Place salmon in skillet and sauté each side for 4 to 5 minutes or until fish is just cooked through. Place cooked fish on warm individual serving plates. Serve with fresh lemon wedges and garnish with cilantro or basil leaves.

ORANGE ROUGHY WITH RASPBERRY SAUCE

Servings: 2

You can replace orange roughy with fresh fillets of red snapper, sole, flounder or any member of the cod family.

½ cup fresh raspberries or blackberries
1 tbs. chopped fresh parsley
1 tbs. white wine
⅛ tsp. sugar
½ tsp. light soy sauce
½ tsp. fresh lemon juice

4 fish fillets, 4 oz. each
2 tbs. olive oil
¼ tsp. garlic powder
¼ tsp. onion powder
¼ tsp. dried thyme
1 tbs. butter

In a small bowl, combine raspberries, parsley, white wine, sugar, soy sauce and lemon juice. Mash raspberries and mix well. Pour into a small saucepan, stir frequently and cook over medium-low heat for 5 to 8 minutes. While sauce thickens, rinse fish and pat dry. Brush fish with 1 tbs. of the oil. Sprinkle both sides of fish with garlic powder, onion powder and thyme. Heat 1½ tsp. oil with 1½ tsp. butter in a skillet over medium heat. Add 2 of the fillets and cook for 4 to 5 minutes on each side or until thickest section is opaque when you cut into it with a knife. Heat remaining oil and melt remaining butter in skillet; sauté remaining 2 fillets. Place fish on warm individual serving plates and top with a layer of raspberry sauce.

VEGETABLE OCEAN FISH SAUTÉ

If you were to try only one recipe from this seafood collection, this is it! The flavor is unbelievable — one of the best fish dishes you will ever taste. Just about any fresh ocean fish will work in this recipe including swordfish, bass or snapper. Stir with a gentle hand if you use a delicate-textured fish such as cod, perch or haddock.

½ lb. fresh ocean fish fillets
2 tbs. butter
2 tbs. olive or canola oil
1 clove garlic, minced or pressed
2 tbs. finely chopped, peeled green chile
  pepper

1 small onion, finely chopped
1 cup diced potato
juice of ½ lemon
¼ tsp. dried thyme
⅛ tsp. pepper
fresh parsley or cilantro sprigs for garnish

Rinse fish and pat dry. Cut fish into 1-inch chunks. Melt butter and heat oil in a skillet over medium-high heat. Add garlic and sauté for 2 minutes or until lightly golden brown. Add chopped peppers, onion and potato. Reduce heat to medium. Cover and cook for 13 to 14 minutes or until potato is tender. Stir occasionally. Add lemon juice, thyme and pepper. Gently stir in fish. Cook uncovered for 4 to 6 minutes or until chunks of fish are cooked. Transfer to individual shallow bowls. Garnish with sprigs of parsley or cilantro.

PAN-GRILLED HALIBUT WITH DELICATE RASPBERRY CRUST

Servings: 2

You'll need an ovenproof skillet with a solid metal handle to prepare this mouth-watering recipe. It's an easy, but sophisticated, dish you can serve to guests, with fresh steamed vegetables and wild rice.

2 halibut fish fillets, 6-8 oz. each, or
  other firm fresh fish
3 tbs. raspberry preserves
2 tsp. fresh lemon juice

¼ cup seasoned breadcrumbs
1 tbs. butter, melted
1 tbs. plus 1 tsp. canola or olive oil
1 tbs. plus 1 tsp. butter

Rinse fish and pat dry. In a small saucepan, combine raspberry preserves and lemon juice. Heat over medium-low. Stir well and reduce to a simmer. In a shallow bowl, mix together breadcrumbs and 1 tbs. melted butter. Set aside. Heat oil with butter in an ovenproof skillet over medium-high heat. Add fish and sauté for 4 to 5 minutes on each side or until fish flakes easily when poked with a fork. Spread a layer of breadcrumb mixture over each fillet. Slowly pour raspberry sauce over breadcrumbs in a series of zig-zag lines to create an interesting presentation. Place skillet under the broiler for 1 minute or until breadcrumbs turn light golden brown. Serve at once on individual serving plates.

POULTRY SAUTÉS

CHICKEN MARSALA

This eye-appealing dish is loaded with luscious flavors, and always a hit with a crowd — just double or triple. It's good with fresh steamed vegetables.

2 chicken breast halves, skinned and
  boned
¼ cup flour
⅛ tsp. pepper
⅛ tsp. salt
2 tbs. butter

½ lb. mushrooms, sliced
2 tbs. olive or canola oil
1 clove garlic, minced or pressed
½ cup chicken broth
½ cup Marsala wine
1 tbs. cornstarch

Rinse chicken and pat dry. Cut chicken into 1½- to 2½-inch pieces. In a shallow bowl, mix together flour, pepper and salt. Dredge chicken in flour mixture, coating all sides. Melt 1 tbs. of the butter in a skillet. Add mushrooms and sauté over medium heat for 4 to 5 minutes or until mushrooms are soft. Remove mushrooms from skillet and set aside. Heat remaining butter and oil in skillet over medium-high heat. Brown chicken for 2 minutes on each side. Remove chicken from skillet. Reduce heat to low. Add garlic, chicken broth and Marsala wine to skillet. Stir well. To prevent clumping, very slowly whisk in cornstarch until well blended. Return chicken and mushrooms to skillet and sauté for 2 to 3 minutes over medium heat or until chicken is cooked through. Serve on a large platter or individual serving plates.

SAVORY CHICKEN SAUTÉ

Servings: 2

You'll need to cook this recipe in an ovenproof skillet with a solid metal body and handle that can withstand a high temperature and open flame. A green garden salad and fresh rolls make perfect accompaniments.

2 chicken breast halves, skinned and boned
1/4 cup skim milk
1/4 cup seasoned breadcrumbs
1 tbs. olive or canola oil
1 tbs. butter
1 clove garlic, minced or pressed
1/4 tsp. dried basil
1/4 tsp. dried oregano
1/4 tsp. dried thyme
1/8 tsp. dried rosemary
1/8 tsp. pepper
2 tbs. dry sherry
2 slices Swiss cheese
4 tomato slices, 1/8-inch thick

Rinse chicken and pat dry. Pour milk into a shallow dish and dip chicken in milk. Coat each side of chicken with breadcrumbs and shake off excess. Heat oil in a skillet and sauté chicken over medium-high heat for 4 to 5 minutes on each side. While chicken is cooking, melt butter in a small saucepan. Add garlic, basil, oregano, thyme, rosemary, pepper and sherry, and cook for 1 minute over medium-low heat. Leave chicken in skillet. Top each chicken breast with a slice of Swiss cheese. Top cheese with tomato slices. Pour savory garlic sauce over tomato slices. Preheat broiler. Place skillet under broiler for 2 to 3 minutes or until cheese has melted. Transfer chicken to individual serving plates. Serve immediately.

CHICKEN ITALIANO

Servings: 2

The secret to this recipe is the addition of Parmesan cheese to the breadcrumb mixture. Always purchase freshly grated Parmesan cheese; the flavor is superior to the processed brands. Use your favorite tomato sauce, or try our recipe on the next page. Serve remaining sauce over pasta. Complete your meal with vegetables and hot Italian garlic bread.

2 chicken breast halves, skinned and
  boned
1/4 cup seasoned breadcrumbs
1 tbs. freshly grated Parmesan cheese
1/4 tsp. dried basil
1/8 tsp. pepper
1 tbs. butter

1 tbs. olive oil
1 egg, beaten
1 clove garlic, minced
2 cups *Italian Tomato Sauce*, follows
1/3 cup shredded mozzarella cheese
1/2 tsp. chopped fresh parsley, or 1/8 tsp.
  dried

Rinse chicken and pat dry. Place chicken between 2 sheets of waxed paper or parchment paper and pound with a meat mallet. In a shallow bowl, combine breadcrumbs, Parmesan cheese, 1/8 tsp. of the basil, and pepper. Melt butter with oil in a skillet over medium-high heat. Dip chicken into egg and coat with breadcrumb mixture. Sauté chicken for 5 to 6 minutes on each side. Remove chicken from skillet.

Sauté garlic for 1 minute over medium heat. Add sauce and remaining $\frac{1}{8}$ tsp. basil. Stir and simmer until hot. Arrange chicken in skillet with sauce; cover and simmer for 10 minutes. Top chicken breasts with mozzarella cheese and sprinkle with parsley. Cover and heat until cheese melts.

ITALIAN TOMATO SAUCE
Yield: 6 cups

Our all-time favorite — a flavorful tomato sauce with a versatile, robust flavor that's perfect with pasta as well as many other dishes.

2 tbs. olive oil
2 cloves garlic, minced or pressed
2 cans (28 oz. each) Italian plum
  tomatoes, chopped and mashed
$\frac{1}{2}$ tsp. dried basil
$\frac{1}{2}$ tsp. dried thyme

$\frac{1}{2}$ tsp. dried oregano
$\frac{1}{2}$ tsp. sugar
$\frac{1}{8}$ tsp. salt
$\frac{1}{4}$ tsp. pepper
1 bay leaf

Heat oil in a medium ($2\frac{1}{2}$- to $3\frac{1}{3}$-quart) saucepan. Add garlic and sauté over medium heat for 2 to 3 minutes or until garlic is golden. Add tomatoes. Stir in basil, thyme, oregano, sugar, salt, pepper and bay leaf. Partially cover saucepan. Raise heat to medium-high until sauce begins to bubble. Reduce heat to low and simmer for at least 3 hours. Stir occasionally. Remove bay leaf and discard.

SIMPLY ELEGANT CHICKEN SAUTÉ

Servings: 2

The zest, also known as the rind, of a lemon is where you'll find the highly aromatic and flavorful oils. A handy and relatively inexpensive kitchen gadget called a lemon zester allows you to easily remove the zest without the bitter white membrane under the lemon skin. Serve with rice.

2 chicken breast halves, skinned and boned
1/4 cup skim milk
1/4 cup flour
1 tbs. butter
1 tbs. olive or canola oil
juice of 1/2 lemon
1/4 cup chicken broth
1/2 tsp. grated fresh lemon rind (zest)
1 tsp. dried dill weed
1/8 tsp. pepper
fresh parsley springs and lemon slices for garnish

Rinse chicken and pat dry. Place chicken between 2 sheets of waxed paper or parchment paper and pound with a meat mallet. Dip chicken into skim milk and dredge with flour; shake off excess. Melt butter with oil in a skillet over medium-high heat. Brown both sides of chicken and cook for about 4 minutes on each side. Remove chicken from skillet and place on warm serving plates. With remaining butter and oil in skillet, add lemon juice, chicken broth, lemon rind, dill weed and pepper. Heat over medium-high heat until hot. Use a spatula to scrape browned bits from skillet to flavor sauce. Spoon sauce over cooked chicken. Garnish with sprigs of parsley and slices of lemon.

QUICK AND EASY CHICKEN PICCATA

This matches nicely with steamed vegetables and rice. For best results, be sure to heat the oil and butter for at least 1 minute before you start sautéing.

4 chicken breast halves, skinned and
  boned
1/8 tsp. salt
1/4 tsp. pepper
1/2 cup plus 1 tbs. flour
1/2 cup skim milk
2 tbs. butter

1 tbs. olive or canola oil
juice of 1/2 lemon
1/2 cup sherry
1 tbs. chopped fresh parsley, or 1 tsp.
  dried for garnish
1 lemon, thinly sliced for garnish

Rinse chicken and pat dry. Fillet each chicken breast into 2 thin cutlets. Tenderize each cutlet with a meat mallet. Combine salt, pepper and 1/2 cup flour in a shallow bowl. Dip cutlets in milk and dredge in flour mixture. Melt 1 tbs. of the butter with oil in a skillet over medium-high heat. Sauté chicken cutlets for 2 to 3 minutes on each side, or until chicken is cooked through. Place chicken on warm serving plates. Add remaining butter, lemon juice and sherry to skillet. Slowly and carefully whisk in remaining flour until flour is no longer visible and sauce bubbles and thickens. Pour sauce over chicken. Garnish with fresh parsley and lemon slices; serve immediately.

SAUTÉED CHICKEN WITH SUN-DRIED TOMATOES

In a hurry? Here's a stunning recipe that's big on flavor but takes just a little bit of time to prepare. Serve with a side of fresh pasta.

2 chicken breast halves, skinned and boned
1 egg, beaten
2 tbs. milk
1/4 cup breadcrumbs
1/4 tsp. garlic powder
1/2 tsp. dried thyme
1/2 tsp. dried basil
1/4 tsp. freshly ground pepper
3 tbs. olive oil
2 tbs. minced sun-dried tomatoes, reconstituted or packed in oil
2 tbs. chopped green bell pepper
1/8 tsp. chopped fresh parsley, or dried
4 lemon wedges

Rinse chicken and pat dry. Combine egg and milk in a shallow bowl, In another shallow bowl, combine breadcrumbs, garlic, thyme, basil and pepper. Heat oil in a skillet over medium-high heat. Dip chicken into egg-milk mixture and coat with breadcrumbs. Shake off excess. Sauté chicken until one side is done, about 8 to 10 minutes. Turn chicken over and top with sun-dried tomato pieces and chopped peppers. Cook for 8 to 10 minutes or until chicken is thoroughly cooked. Place chicken on individual serving plates. Sprinkle with parsley. Serve with lemon wedges.

CREAMY MUSHROOM CHICKEN

Servings: 2

Every cookbook should be allowed at least one cream of mushroom soup recipe! This one is so quick and easy, and so good, we've slipped it in. Serve this old-fashioned standard during the cold winter months. Pour the extra sauce over a vegetable side dish, such as string beans.

2 chicken breast halves, with bones and skin
1 tbs. olive or canola oil
½ cup chopped celery
¼ cup chopped onion
¼ tsp. dried thyme
¼ tsp. pepper
1 can (10¾ oz.) cream of mushroom soup
1 cup skim milk
cooked rice

Rinse chicken and pat dry. Parboil chicken for 10 minutes. Heat oil in a preheated skillet over medium heat. Add celery and onion; sauté for 4 to 5 minutes or until soft. Add thyme, pepper, soup and milk. Stir until well blended. Add chicken, cover and cook over low heat for 30 minutes. Turn chicken frequently. Serve chicken with sauce over a bed of rice on individual serving plates.

CHICKEN WITH RED RASPBERRIES

Servings: 2

The dish looks, tastes and smells irresistible. Purchase freshly picked raspberries that are bright, dry and plump. Once picked, these fragile and delicate berries will only stay fresh for up to 2 days. Fortunately raspberries freeze exceptionally well, and thawed raspberries are fine for cooking.

2 chicken breast halves, skinned and boned
1 tbs. olive or canola oil
$1/4$ cup red raspberry preserves
2 tbs. white wine
$1/2$ cup fresh or frozen, thawed raspberries
$1/8$ tsp. dried mint

Rinse chicken and pat dry. Slice chicken breast into $1/4$-inch-thick medallions. Heat oil in a skillet over medium-high heat. Sauté chicken for 2 to 3 minutes on each side. While chicken is cooking, combine preserves and white wine in a small saucepan and heat over low heat. Place chicken on warm serving plates and top with warm raspberry sauce. Scatter raspberries over chicken and sprinkle with mint. Serve immediately.

SAUTÉED CHICKEN BREAST WITH ZESTY PECAN SAUCE

For best results, the thickness of the chicken breast should be uniform before cooking. A ½-inch-thick chicken breast will measure ¼ inch after it has been well pounded. This enables the chicken to cook quickly, producing a tender, perfectly flavored result. Serve this dish with steamed vegetables and wild rice.

2 chicken breast halves, skinned and
  boned
¼ cup skim milk
¼ cup flour
1 tbs. butter

1 tbs. olive or canola oil
Zesty Pecan Sauce, follows
fresh cilantro or thyme sprigs for
  garnish

Rinse chicken and pat dry. Place chicken between 2 sheets of waxed paper or parchment paper and pound with a meat mallet. Dip chicken into skim milk. Dredge chicken in flour and shake off excess. Heat butter and oil in a skillet over medium-high heat. Add chicken and brown quickly to sear. Sauté for about 4 minutes on each side. Remove chicken from skillet and set aside on warm serving plates. Spread *Zesty Pecan Sauce* over chicken breast. Garnish with sprigs of cilantro or thyme.

ZESTY PECAN SAUCE

3 tbs. butter
¼ cup chopped pecans
1 tbs. white vinegar

1 tbs. fresh lemon juice
1 tbs. fresh lime juice
⅛ tsp. dried parsley

Melt 3 tbs. butter in same skillet. Add pecans and cook for 1 minute. Remove pecans from skillet. Combine vinegar, lemon and lime juices and parsley in skillet. Cook for 1 minute over medium heat. Add pecans to skillet. Stir thoroughly.

WALNUT HERB CHICKEN OASIS

Servings: 2

This satisfying recipe with subtle herb and nut flavor is quick and easy to follow.

2 chicken breast halves, skinned and boned
3 tbs. walnut pieces or halves
1½ tbs. olive or canola oil
1 clove garlic, minced or pressed
1 tbs. fresh lemon juice
1 tbs. fresh lime juice
1 small sweet Vidalia onion, diced

2 medium tomatoes, peeled and cut into wedges
¼ cup red, yellow or green bell pepper strips, matchstick size
¼ cup chopped fresh basil
⅛ tsp. salt
¼ tsp. pepper
steamed white rice, optional

Rinse chicken, pat dry and cut into 1-inch cubes. In a dry nonstick skillet, heat walnuts over medium-low heat, stirring constantly, until light golden brown. Remove from skillet and set aside. Heat 1 tbs. of the oil in skillet over medium heat. Add garlic and sauté for 1 minute. Add chicken pieces and sauté until cooked through. Remove from skillet and set aside. Over medium-high heat, add lemon and lime juices, remaining ½ tbs. oil, onion, tomato wedges and bell pepper. Cover and cook for 4 minutes. Stir occasionally. Add chicken, basil, walnuts, salt and pepper. Cook until chicken is hot. Serve immediately on individual serving plates or a platter with rice.

SAUTÉED BARBECUED CHICKEN TIPS

This recipe makes an appetizing and spicy meal. Serve with rice pilaf or, for a change, on bulky rolls for great-tasting sandwiches.

1 lb. chicken breast halves or thighs,
  skinned and boned
2 tbs. canola or olive oil

1/4 tsp. freshly ground pepper
Barbecue Sauce, follows

Rinse chicken and pat dry. Cut into 1-x-2-inch pieces. Heat oil in a skillet over medium-high heat. Add chicken pieces and pepper and sauté for 3 to 4 minutes. Add *Barbecue Sauce* and sauté, stirring frequently, for 3 minutes or until chicken is cooked through.

BARBECUE SAUCE
1/4 cup ketchup
2 tbs. Worcestershire sauce
2 tbs. vinegar
2 tbs. water
1 tbs. finely chopped onion

1 tbs. brown sugar
1/4 tsp. chili powder
1/2 tsp. dry mustard
dash cayenne pepper
1 clove garlic, minced or pressed

Combine all ingredients in a saucepan and mix well. Simmer for 20 minutes over medium-low heat. Stir occasionally.

SEASONED CHICKEN WITH RED WINE

Servings: 4

The blend of dried brown mustard with other seasonings adds a pungent flavor to this chicken dish.

4 chicken breast halves, skinned and
  boned
1/3 cup flour
1/2 tsp. pepper
1/2 tsp. dry brown mustard
1/2 tsp. paprika
1/2 tsp. dried thyme
1/4 tsp. dried rosemary
1/2 tsp. dried sage

1/2 tsp. dried marjoram
1/2 cup skim milk
1 tbs. butter
1 clove garlic, minced or pressed
2 medium yellow onions, peeled, cut
  into wedges, separated
1/2 cup dry red wine
1/4 tsp. dried basil
1/4 tsp. dried oregano

Rinse chicken and pat dry. In a shallow bowl, combine flour, pepper, brown mustard, paprika, thyme, rosemary, sage and marjoram. Mix well. Dip chicken in milk and dredge in flour mixture. Melt butter in a deep-sided sauté pan over medium heat. Add garlic and sauté for 1 minute. Add chicken and brown all sides. Surround chicken with separated onion wedges and pour in red wine. Sprinkle with basil and oregano. Cover and reduce heat to medium-low. Simmer for 20 minutes or until chicken is cooked through.

SAUTÉED CHICKEN WITH APPLES AND SNOW PEAS

Servings: 2

Use freshly picked pea pods for a bright green color, crisp texture and a sugar-sweet flavor. Serve with red-skinned potatoes or rice and a fresh salad.

2 chicken breast halves, skinned and
  boned
½ lb. fresh pea pods
1 tbs. olive or canola oil
1 large sweet onion, thinly sliced
1 large firm tart apple, cored, peeled
  and cut into thick wedges

2 tbs. Dijon mustard
1 tbs. fresh lemon juice
¼ tsp. pepper
2 tsp. toasted sesame seeds, optional

Rinse chicken, pat dry and cut into 1-inch-wide strips. Trim off stems and remove threads from pea pods. Blanch pods in a pot of boiling water for 2 to 3 minutes. Drain and plunge into cold water. Set aside. Heat oil in a skillet over medium heat. Add onion and sauté for 3 to 4 minutes. Add chicken strips and sauté for 3 minutes. Add apple wedges, mustard, lemon juice and pepper. Mix thoroughly. Cover and cook for 4 minutes, stirring occasionally. Stir in pea pods and sesame seeds. Sauté uncovered for 1 more minute or until pea pods are heated through and chicken is cooked.

CHICKEN WITH HERBS AND WHITE WINE

Servings: 2

In this recipe it's ok to eliminate the jalapeño peppers; it's equally as tasty but just not as intensely spicy. Serve with wild rice or over pasta.

2 chicken breast halves, skinned and boned
1 tbs. plus 1 tsp. olive or canola oil
1/4 tsp. pepper
1/4 tsp. dried oregano
1/4 tsp dried thyme
3/4 cup sliced white mushrooms
1 red bell pepper, cut into 1/4-inch strips

1 tsp. minced jalapeño pepper
1 can (2.25 oz.) black olives, sliced
1 small onion, diced
1/4 tsp. dried basil
1/8 tsp. salt
3/4 cup white wine
1 cup chicken broth
1 cup tomato paste

Rinse chicken and pat dry. Rub chicken with 1 tsp. of the oil and season with 1/8 tsp. of the pepper. Heat remaining 1 tbs. oil in a skillet over medium heat, and add oregano and thyme. Add chicken and sauté on each side for 4 to 5 minutes. Remove from skillet and set aside. Add mushrooms, peppers, olives and onion. Season with remaining 1/8 tsp. pepper, basil and salt. Sauté for 8 to 10 minutes. Stir occasionally. Add white wine, chicken broth and tomato paste. Mix and heat well. Return chicken to skillet; surround and top chicken with vegetables. Cover skillet, reduce heat to low and simmer for 20 minutes. Place chicken and vegetables on serving plates.

QUICK AND EASY CHICKEN CACCIATORE

Servings: 4

This is an easily prepared version of a favorite Italian specialty.

1 tbs. olive oil
4 chicken breast halves or thighs,
  skinned and boned
1 medium onion, chopped
1 clove garlic, minced or pressed
1 cup sliced mushrooms
½ medium red bell pepper, diced
½ medium green bell pepper, diced
1 cup tomato sauce

2 cups diced fresh tomatoes
½ cup chicken broth
¼ tsp. dried basil
¼ tsp. dried oregano
⅛ tsp. salt
¼ tsp. pepper
1 tbs. minced fresh parsley

Rinse chicken and pat dry. Heat oil in a skillet over medium-high heat. Brown chicken on both sides. Add onion, garlic, mushrooms and peppers. Sauté for 2 to 3 minutes. Add tomato sauce, tomato pieces, chicken broth, basil, oregano, salt and pepper. Mix well. Reduce heat to low, cover and simmer for 20 to 25 minutes or until done. Serve on a platter or individual plates. Sprinkle with fresh parsley.

CHICKEN FAJITAS

Be sure to keep your hands away from your eyes after handling a jalapeño pepper. If the potent juices get into your eyes, it is extremely painful.

4 chicken breast halves, skinned and boned
3 tbs. olive oil
2 tbs. fresh lime juice
2 tbs. fresh lemon juice
1/4 tsp. dried thyme

1/4 tsp. dried basil
1/2 tsp. pepper
1 jalapeño pepper, ribs and seeds removed, finely chopped
1 red bell pepper, cut into thin strips
8 large corn or flour tortillas, warmed

Rinse chicken and pat dry. Slice chicken into long strips 1/2-inch wide. In a small bowl, combine 2 tbs. of the olive oil, lime and lemon juices, thyme, basil and pepper. Mix well. Add chicken, cover and refrigerate for 2 hours. Heat remaining 1 tbs. oil in a preheated large skillet over medium heat. Add jalapeño and sauté for 1 minute. Add red bell pepper and sauté for 2 more minutes. Remove pepper from pan and set aside. Add chicken with sauce to skillet and sauté for 2 to 3 minutes or until chicken is cooked through. Serve with warm tortillas and sautéed peppers.

SAUTÉED CHICKEN SALAD

Serve as a salad dish for lunch or as a filling for great sandwiches.

2 chicken breast halves, skinned and
  boned
1 tbs. olive or canola oil
1/4 tsp. dried basil
1/4 tsp. dried oregano
1/8 tsp. pepper
1/2 cup plain low fat yogurt
1/2 tsp. dry mustard

1 tsp. fresh lemon juice
1 tbs. balsamic vinegar
1/8 tsp. salt
1/3 cup finely chopped red bell pepper
1/3 cup finely chopped carrot
1/4 cup finely chopped sweet yellow onion
1 stalk celery, finely chopped
Boston red leaf lettuce

Rinse chicken, pat dry and cut into 1/2-inch strips. Heat oil in a skillet over medium heat. Add chicken, sprinkle with basil, oregano and pepper, and sauté for 7 or 8 minutes or until chicken is cooked. Remove from heat and let cool. In a large bowl, combine yogurt, dry mustard, lemon juice, vinegar and salt; mix well. Add red pepper, carrot, onion, celery and chicken. Mix well. Cover 2 individual serving plates with lettuce and top with chicken mixture. Serve chilled.

TURKEY CUTLETS WITH ORANGE SAUCE

To add a nice touch, garnish this dish with decorative orange slices. Serve with oven-roasted potatoes and fresh green vegetables.

4 turkey cutlets, 4-6 oz. each
1/4 cup flour
1 tsp. dried thyme
1/8 tsp. salt
1/4 tsp. pepper
1 tbs. olive oil
2 tbs. butter
1/4 cup minced shallots

1 cup fresh orange juice
1 tsp. grated fresh orange rind (zest)
2 tbs. fresh lemon juice
1/2 tsp. grated fresh lemon rind (zest)
1 tsp. cornstarch
fresh thyme sprigs for garnish
orange slices for garnish

Rinse turkey and pat dry. In a shallow bowl, combine flour, thyme, salt and pepper. Dredge turkey cutlets in flour mixture. Heat oil in a skillet over medium heat. Add cutlets and sauté for 6 to 7 minutes on each side or until turkey is cooked through. Place turkey on 4 warm individual serving plates and set aside. Wipe skillet clean with a paper towel. Heat 2 tbs. butter in a skillet over medium heat. Add shallots and sauté for 1 minute. Add orange and lemon juices and zests; whisk in cornstarch. Bring to a boil. Reduce heat and simmer for 3 minutes. Pour sauce over turkey and garnish with sprigs of thyme and orange slices.

NEW AMERICAN SLOPPY JOES

Here's our white meat alternative to the traditional red meat "Sloppy Joe." Kids and adults go wild over these luscious sandwiches.

1 tbs. olive or canola oil
1 clove garlic, minced or pressed
1 small onion, minced
1 large green bell pepper, diced
1/4 lb. mushrooms, diced
1 lb. ground turkey
1/3 cup tomato sauce

1/2 cup ketchup
1 tbs. Worcestershire sauce
1/2 tsp. dried basil
1/2 tsp. pepper
1/2 tsp. dried oregano
pita bread or buns

Heat oil in a skillet. Add garlic, onion, pepper and mushrooms; sauté over medium heat for 5 to 6 minutes or until vegetables are soft. Remove vegetables from skillet and set aside. Heat skillet over medium heat. Add ground turkey and sauté for 5 to 6 minutes, stirring frequently, or until turkey is crumbled and cooked through. Drain. Stir in tomato sauce, ketchup, Worcestershire sauce and cooked vegetables. Sprinkle with basil, pepper and oregano. Mix well. Cook over low heat for 7 minutes. Stir occasionally. Serve in pita pockets or on buns.

MEAT SAUTÉS

SAUTÉED SIRLOIN STEAKS

Servings: 2

Here's a hearty entrée for the meat-and-potatoes person. The flawless recipe for the sauce is easy to create and adds a smashing flavor to the beef.

1 tbs. vegetable oil
¼ tsp. pepper
⅛ tsp. salt
¼ tsp. grated fresh lemon rind (zest)
2 sirloin steaks, 6 oz. each
½ cup beef broth

1 tbs. red wine or sherry
2 tbs. fresh lemon juice
2 tsp. cornstarch
1 tsp. dried parsley
⅛ tsp. dried rosemary

In a small bowl, combine oil, pepper, salt and lemon rind. Mix well. Rinse steaks and pat dry. Brush steaks on both sides with oil mixture. Preheat a skillet over medium-high heat. Sear steaks on both sides. Reduce heat and sauté until done to your desire. Place steaks on warm serving plates and cover to keep warm. Add beef broth, wine, lemon juice and cornstarch to skillet. Mix well and bring to a quick boil. Stir in parsley and rosemary. Scrape browned bits from bottom of skillet and blend into sauce. Pour thickened sauce over steaks. Serve immediately.

FILET MIGNON

Sautéing often leaves a thin layer, or "glaze," of browned food particles on the bottom of the pan. To "deglaze" a pan, add a little liquid, (¼ cup to ½ cup) such as beef or chicken broth, wine, sherry or a combination. Heat over medium-high heat and scrape the bottom of the pan to remove the cooked browned particles. Reduce the liquid by half or until it thickens and pour it over your cooked foods. To protect your cookware, do not use a skillet with a nonstick coating when deglazing. However, a hard anodized skillet is ideal for this job.

Try a butterfly cut for thick pieces of meat when cooking for medium to well done. To butterfly, slice beef horizontally by placing it flat on a cutting board and cut it almost into 2 thin slices. Stop cutting at the last inch so the 2 pieces remain intact. Fold beef open and cook.

1 tbs. plus 1 tsp. butter
2 small sweet yellow onions, thinly
  sliced and separated into rings
½ lb. white mushrooms, sliced
½ tsp. pepper
¼ tsp. dried basil
¼ tsp. dried thyme

2 tsp. olive oil
2 filets mignon, 8 oz. each, 2 inches
  thick
⅓ cup dry sherry
¼ cup beef broth
Bearnaise Sauce, optional, page 56

Melt 1 tbs. of the butter in a skillet over medium heat. Add onions and sauté for 2 minutes. Add mushrooms and sauté for an additional 5 minutes. Transfer from pan to 2 warm ovenproof serving plates and place in a preheated 225° oven. In a small bowl, combine pepper, basil and thyme. Rub 1 tsp. of the oil over filets and sprinkle with pepper mixture. Heat remaining 1 tsp. oil and 1 tsp. butter in a preheated skillet over medium-high heat. Place filets in skillet and sauté for 3 minutes. Carefully turn filets over and cook to your desire. Use an instant-read thermometer to check for doneness: rare 130 F, medium 140 F, well done 160 F. Remove filets from skillet and place on onions and mushrooms. Pour sherry and beef broth into skillet, and with a straight-edged metal spatula, scrape browned bits from bottom of skillet. Stir frequently and cook until sauce is reduced by half. Pour sauce from skillet over filets and serve. For additional flavor, top with *Bearnaise Sauce*.

BEARNAISE SAUCE

Sinfully delicious and fairly easy to prepare. Serve warm over cooked slices of beef, chicken or fish.

2 tbs. white wine vinegar
2 tbs. white wine
1 small green or yellow onion, finely
  chopped
1 tbs. chopped fresh tarragon or parsley

3 egg yolks, room temperature
2 tbs. water, room temperature
6 oz. butter
dash cayenne pepper

In a very small saucepan, combine vinegar, wine, onion and tarragon. Cook over medium heat until reduced by half, about 2 tablespoons. Remove from heat and let cool. Over low heat in a double boiler, whip egg yolks, water and tarragon mixture until creamy. Cut butter into 1/2-inch slices and add to sauce 1 piece at a time, allowing butter to slowly melt in sauce each time, while continuously whipping with a whisk. As butter melts, eggs will cook and thicken sauce. Pour sauce into a stainless steel or ceramic gravy boat. Sprinkle with cayenne pepper and serve immediately.

SAUTÉED BEEF WITH MUSTARD SAUCE

You can serve this over rice or noodles, or on a bulky roll for outstanding sandwiches.

1 lb. sirloin or flank steak
1 tbs. plus 2 tsp. butter
1 tbs. plus 2 tsp. olive oil
2 tbs. minced onion
2 cups sliced mushrooms

½ cup beef broth
2 tsp. Dijon mustard
2 tbs. Worcestershire sauce
2 tsp. cornstarch
cooked rice or noodles, optional

Cut beef across the grain into ⅛-inch thick slices 2½ inches long. Melt 2 tsp. of the butter with 2 tsp. of the oil in a skillet over medium heat. Add onion and mushrooms; sauté for 6 minutes. Transfer mushroom-onion mixture to a bowl and set aside. Melt remaining 1 tbs. butter with remaining 1 tbs. oil in skillet over medium-high heat. Add beef and sauté for 3 to 5 minutes or until cooked to your desire. Remove beef from skillet and set aside. Combine beef broth, mustard, Worcestershire sauce and cornstarch in skillet over medium heat; mix well. Scrape browned bits from pan and blend into sauce. Add reserved mushroom-onion mixture and beef to sauce after it thickens and reduces. Mix well and heat. Serve over rice or noodles if desired.

SKILLET HAMBURGERS

Our mission was to create the ultimate burger. This is it! Just right. Not overpowering but full of flavor.

1 lb. ground beef, chuck or round
¼ tsp. pepper
⅛ tsp. salt
1 tsp. Worcestershire sauce
2 tbs. butter

1 tbs. vegetable oil
2 tbs. finely chopped scallions
¼ cup sherry
1 tbs. chopped red onion
bulky roll, fresh loaf or pita bread

Gently mix meat with pepper, salt and Worcestershire sauce. Shape beef mixture into 4 patties ¾-inch thick. Melt 1 tbs. of the butter with oil in a skillet over medium-high heat. Place burgers in skillet and sear on both sides. Reduce heat to medium and cook to desired doneness. Remove burgers from skillet and place on warm plates. Add scallions to skillet and sauté for 1 minute. Pour in sherry and add remaining 1 tbs. butter. Scrape browned bits from pan and blend into liquid. Reduce sauce by ⅓ and pour over burgers. Top with chopped red onion and serve on bread of choice.

SAUTÉED LIVER AND ONIONS

You can find frozen liver in your supermarket. It's individually packaged in ¼-pound slices, ideal for preparing this recipe.

¼ cup olive oil
1 large sweet onion, sliced
½ lb. sliced beef liver, thawed
¼ tsp. salt
¼ tsp. pepper

Heat oil in a skillet over medium-high heat. Add onion slices and sauté until soft. Push onions to one side of skillet. Add liver and brown on each side. Reduce heat to low. Sprinkle with salt and pepper; cover and cook until done. Place liver on individual serving plates covered with onions.

STUFFED VEAL CUTLETS

You can substitute very thinly pounded turkey or chicken cutlets in place of veal. This is good served with pasta.

½ cup cooked chopped broccoli
¾ cup ricotta cheese
3 tbs. grated Parmesan cheese
½ tsp. dried basil
2 tbs. chopped walnuts
⅛ tsp. salt
⅛ tsp. pepper

3 thin slices prosciutto
1 lb. veal cutlets, about ¼-⅓-inch thick
1 tbs. olive oil
1 tbs. butter
1 cup chicken broth
1 tbs. fresh lemon juice
chopped fresh or dried parsley for garnish

Combine broccoli, ricotta cheese, Parmesan cheese, basil, walnuts, salt and pepper in a food processor and mix well. Place a slice of prosciutto on top of each cutlet. Spread ⅓ of the ricotta mixture down the center of each cutlet, covering prosciutto. Roll up each cutlet lengthwise and secure with string. Heat oil and butter in a skillet over medium heat. Brown veal on all sides. Add chicken broth and lemon juice. Cover and cook for 10 minutes. Place veal rolls on individual serving plates and top with remaining sauce. Sprinkle with parsley and serve.

SAUTÉED VEAL SCALOPPINE

Servings: 2

A perfect balance of flavors allows you to enjoy the seasonings without masking the flavor of the veal. A subtle sauce makes an elegant dish. Serve with pasta and vegetables.

½ lb. veal cutlets
dash salt
dash pepper
1 tbs. butter
1 tbs. olive oil

1 clove garlic, minced or pressed
3 tbs. white wine
¼ tsp. dried oregano
1 tsp. chopped fresh parsley for garnish

Pound cutlets with a meat mallet until ⅛-inch thick. Sprinkle salt and pepper on both sides of cutlet. Melt butter with oil in a skillet over medium heat. Sauté veal for 2 minutes or until golden brown. Turn veal over and sauté for 2 more minutes. Place veal on a warm plate. Add garlic to skillet and sauté for 1 minute. Add wine and oregano to skillet and boil for 2 to 3 minutes. Use a sharp-edged spatula to scrape off cooked browned bits and blend into sauce. Return veal to skillet and stir with sauce for 30 seconds. Transfer to individual serving plates. Pour sauce over veal and sprinkle with fresh parsley.

SAVORY LAMB SAUTÉ

Slow cooking allows the crisp apple and aromatic herbs to infuse the lamb with a truly spectacular flavor. Serve with rice.

1 Granny Smith apple, peeled, cored and cut into 1/8-inch slices
juice of 1/2 lemon
2 tbs. olive oil
1/2 lb. lamb, cut into 1-inch cubes
1 clove garlic, minced or pressed
1 onion, chopped
1/4 cup dry sherry
2 tsp. honey

1/2 tsp. dried thyme
1/4 tsp. dried rosemary
1/4 tsp. fennel seeds, ground
1/2 tsp. ground turmeric
1/2 tsp. rubbed sage
1/8 tsp. salt
1/4 tsp. pepper
fresh rosemary or mint sprigs for garnish

Combine apple slices in a bowl with fresh lemon juice and set aside. Heat oil in a skillet over medium heat. Brown lamb pieces on all sides. Transfer to a warm plate; leave oil in skillet. Add garlic and onion to skillet and sauté for 2 to 3 minutes or until onion is tender. Add sherry, honey, apples with lemon juice and reserved lamb. Stir in thyme, rosemary, fennel, turmeric, sage, salt and pepper. Cover skillet and reduce heat to low; simmer for 1 1/2 hours. Stir occasionally. Serve on individual plates and garnish with sprigs of rosemary or mint.

TASTY LAMB AND OKRA SAUTÉ

Servings: 2

Commonly used in Mediterranean dishes, okra has become widely available in most supermarkets and can be found in the fresh produce section. Cook with fresh green okra that's 3-4 inches long. Wash the okra with a good vegetable brush before slicing to remove the outside fuzz.

2 tbs. breadcrumbs
2 tbs. grated Parmesan cheese
1/4 tsp. ground cumin
1/4 cup olive oil
1/2 lb. lamb, cut into 1-inch cubes
1 cup water

1/4 cup minced shallots
2 cups sliced okra
1/2 cup chopped onion
1/8 tsp. turmeric
1 tbs. fresh lemon juice

In a shallow bowl, combine breadcrumbs, Parmesan cheese and cumin. Set aside. Heat 1 tbs. of the oil in a preheated skillet over medium-high heat. Add lamb and brown all sides, about 4 to 5 minutes. Add water and shallots. Reduce heat to medium and simmer until most of the liquid cooks down, about 20 minutes. While lamb is cooking, dredge okra slices in breadcrumb mixture. Heat remaining 3 tbs. oil in another skillet over medium heat. Add onion and sauté for 2 minutes. Add okra, turmeric and lemon juice. Sauté for 7 to 10 minutes. Serve on individual serving plates with cooked lamb.

SAUTÉED PORK CHOPS WITH APPLE WEDGES

The rich, full-flavored sauce teams up nicely with pork chops for a different and satisfying recipe.

2 tbs. butter
1 tbs. canola oil
2 pork loin chops, 1-inch thick
2 tbs. chopped shallots
1 cup sliced mushrooms
2 tbs. white wine

1 tbs. orange marmalade
3 tbs. chicken broth
3 tbs. heavy cream
6 Granny Smith apple wedges, about
   $1/8$-inch thick

Melt butter with oil in a skillet over medium-high heat. Add chops and quickly cook on both sides, searing in juices. Reduce heat to medium-low and cook until just cooked through. Place chops on warm serving plates and set aside. In the same skillet over medium heat, add shallots and mushrooms; sauté for 4 to 5 minutes. Add white wine, marmalade and chicken broth. Stir thoroughly and sauté for 1 minute. Pour in heavy cream. Stir constantly until sauce thickens and is bubbling. Cover chops with shallots, mushrooms and sauce. Top each chop with 3 apple wedges laid out in a fan design. Serve immediately.

PORK AND CHEESE ROSTI

A delightful dish. The ground fennel takes center stage as the secret subtle flavor that everyone will ask about. You can have a meal for two; or cut the rosti into wedges and serve it as a side dish for a crowd.

½ lb. Italian sausage
2 tsp. plus 3 tbs. butter
2 large baked potatoes
¾ cup shredded Monterey Jack,
  mozzarella or Swiss cheese

½ tsp. dried thyme
¼ tsp. fennel seeds, ground
¼ tsp. pepper
⅛ tsp. salt

Remove sausage meat from casings and crumble into small pieces. Melt 2 tsp. of the butter in a skillet. Add sausage meat and sauté over medium heat until meat is brown and thoroughly cooked. Remove meat from skillet, set aside and wipe skillet clean. Slice cooked potatoes in half. Coarsely grate potato halves against a grater. Discard skins. In a large bowl, gently combine grated potatoes, cooked sausage meat, ¼ cup shredded cheese, thyme, fennel, pepper and salt. Melt remaining butter in an ovenproof 10-inch skillet. Pour potato mixture into pan and cook for 10 minutes. Press down on potato mixture and flip. Cook for 5 to 7 minutes. Sprinkle top with remaining shredded cheese. Place skillet under a preheated broiler for 2 to 3 minutes or until cheese is melted. Divide in half and serve immediately on warm plates.

BRAISED PORK WITH WHITE WINE AND CLAMS

Servings: 2

The pork and clams create a stylish dish that's just right for a special occasion.

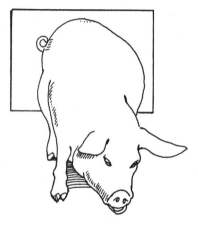

1 lb. boneless pork
1 tbs. canola or olive oil
1 clove garlic, minced
1 tbs. chopped shallots
2 large tomatoes, peeled and diced
3 tbs. tomato paste
1/4 tsp. dried thyme
1 tsp. paprika
1/4 tsp. dried marjoram
1/8 tsp. salt
1/4 tsp. pepper
1 cup white wine

1 lb. small clams in the shell
2 quarts cold water, or more if needed
1 tbs. salt
1/3 tsp. oats
1/2 cup water
1 bay leaf
4 lemon wedges for garnish
1 tbs. chopped fresh parsley for garnish

Cut pork into 1-inch cubes. Heat oil in a skillet over medium-high heat. Add pork and brown all sides. Add garlic, shallots, tomatoes, tomato paste, thyme, paprika, marjoram, salt, pepper and wine. Reduce heat to low and simmer for 1 hour or until pork is cooked through.

While pork is simmering, prepare clams. Be sure all clam shells are closed tightly. Tap shells that are open to see if they will close. Discard all that don't close. Scrub clams under cold running water with a stiff brush. Place in a large pan of cold salted water with oats for 20 minutes. (The clams will ingest the oats and will discharge sand and waste.) Rinse again in cold salted water. Place in a covered saucepan with ½ cup water and 1 bay leaf. Cook for 4 to 5 minutes over high heat until shells open. Discard bay leaf and clams that have not opened after cooking. Drain clams and add to skillet with pork after pork has cooked. Heat for 4 to 5 minutes. Spoon onto individual shallow serving bowls. Garnish with lemon wedges and sprinkle with fresh parsley.

LEMON MUSTARD PORK CHOPS

Servings: 2

This dish has such an exquisite flavor you'll want to serve it next time you have company.

1/4 tsp. pepper
1 tsp. dried thyme
1 tsp. dried coriander
1/4 tsp. onion powder
2 pork loin chops, 1-inch thick, well trimmed

1 tbs. olive oil
2 tbs. minced onion
2 tsp. fresh lemon juice
3 tbs. white wine
1/2 tsp. grated fresh lemon rind (zest)
1 tbs. Dijon mustard

In a small bowl, combine pepper, thyme, coriander and onion powder. Rub pork chops with seasoning mixture. Heat oil in a skillet over medium heat. Add onion and 1 tsp. of the lemon juice; sauté for 3 minutes or until onion is wilted. Add pork chops and sauté on each side for 7 to 8 minutes or until an instant-read thermometer reads 160°. Place chops and onion on warm serving plates. Add wine, remaining 1 tsp. lemon juice, lemon zest and mustard to skillet over medium heat. Stir frequently; scrape and incorporate cooked browned bits from skillet into sauce. After sauce thickens, pour over chops. Serve at once.

SAUTÉED SIDE DISHES AND VEGETARIAN ENTRÉES

FRESH BASIL SAUTÉ

Servings: 4

These combined ingredients, when cooked, will release juices to create a zesty sauce that's perfect to serve with the vegetables over pasta. Perfect as a vegetable side dish, or a vegetarian main course.

2 medium yellow croockneck or zucchini squash
1/4 cup olive oil
2 tbs. fresh lemon juice
1/2 tsp. red pepper flakes
1 tbs. pine nuts
1/2 cup coarsely chopped fresh basil
2 large tomatoes, skins removed, cut into 1-inch chunks
1/4 cup grated Parmesan cheese

Slice squash in half lengthwise and remove seeds. Slice squash into 1/4-inch-thick half circles. Heat oil in a skillet over medium heat. Add squash and sauté for 4 minutes or until tender. Add lemon juice, red pepper flakes, pine nuts and basil. Sauté for 3 to 5 minutes. Add tomatoes and cheese. Sauté until tomatoes are warm through and cheese is melted.

SAUTÉED TOMATOES WITH FRESH HERBS

Servings: 4

You can substitute large chunks of other varieties of fresh tomatoes for equally good flavor, but the cherry tomato halves make the best presentation. Serve with seafood, meats or poultry. You'll need an ovenproof skillet with a metal handle to prepare this dish.

1 tbs. breadcrumbs
1 tbs. grated Parmesan cheese
1 tbs. canola oil
1 clove garlic, minced or pressed
12-18 cherry tomatoes, stemmed and halved
½ tsp. balsamic vinegar
1 tbs. chopped fresh basil, oregano or thyme, or a combination

In a small bowl, combine breadcrumbs and Parmesan cheese. Heat oil in an ovenproof skillet over medium heat. Add garlic and sauté for 1 minute. Add tomato halves. Stir frequently and gently for 3 to 4 minutes. Remove skillet from heat. Sprinkle tomatoes with breadcrumb mixture and place ovenproof skillet under a preheated broiler for 2 minutes. Remove skillet from oven. Drizzle tomatoes with vinegar and sprinkle with fresh herbs. Serve immediately.

FRESH CRANBERRY CITRUS SAUTÉ

Servings: 2

For a nice change of pace, serve this beside pork, poultry or beef.

1 tbs. olive or canola oil
1 small sweet onion, minced
½ cup fresh orange juice
1 tbs. grated fresh orange rind (zest)
1 tbs. fresh lemon juice
1 tsp. grated fresh lemon rind (zest)
2 tsp. chopped fresh tarragon, or ½ tsp. dried
⅓ cup "lite" maple syrup
1½ cups fresh cranberries

Heat oil in a skillet over medium heat. Add onion and sauté for 4 minutes. Add orange and lemon juices, zests and tarragon. Stir in syrup and cranberries. Cook for 5 minutes, stirring frequently. Serve warm or at room temperature as a side dish.

LOW FAT FARMSTAND SAUTÉ

Here's a great-tasting healthy dish that's a snap to prepare.

3 tbs. chicken broth
1 clove garlic, minced or pressed
1 medium Vidalia onion or other
  sweet yellow onion, finely chopped
2 small zucchini, sliced into ¼-inch-thick rounds
1 small yellow crookneck squash,
  sliced into ¼-inch-thick rounds
¼ tsp. dried thyme
⅛ tsp. salt
¼ tsp. pepper
1 tbs. grated Parmesan cheese, optional

Heat chicken broth in a large skillet over medium heat. Add garlic and onion and sauté until soft, about 3 to 4 minutes. Add squash, reduce heat to low and sauté for 10 to 12 minutes or until squash is tender. Remove from heat and stir in thyme, salt and pepper. Serve warm. Top with grated Parmesan cheese if desired.

CUCUMBER SAUTÉ

Servings: 4

If you haven't tried sautéing cucumbers, it's a wonderful treat. You can experiment with lots of other seasonings. The cucumbers are loaded with water, so just be sure to cook over moderate temperature for a short period to retain moisture. This recipe is good as a side dish or over sautéed or baked fish.

2 medium cucumbers
2 tbs. butter
1 tbs. minced onion
1 tbs. fresh lemon juice
1/2 tsp. curry powder
1 tbs. chopped fresh basil
1 tbs. chopped fresh dill weed
1/8 tsp. salt
1/4 tsp. pepper

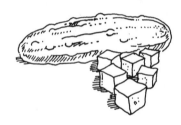

Peel cucumbers, slice in half lengthwise and remove seeds. Cut cucumbers into 1/2-inch to 1-inch cubes. This should yield about 4 cups. Melt butter in a skillet over medium-low heat. Add onion and sauté for 1 minute. Add cucumbers, lemon juice and curry. Stir well. Sprinkle with herbs, salt and pepper. Gently sauté for 4 to 5 minutes. Serve immediately.

FAVORITE HOME FRIES

Servings: 3-4

If you're cooking with new potatoes, there's no need to peel; just scrub the potatoes with a good, stiff vegetable brush. They're not just for breakfast — serve these any time of the day.

4 cups potato cubes, ½-inch-1 inch
¼ tsp. paprika
2 tbs. olive oil
1 cup diced onion
½ tsp. dried rosemary

¼ tsp. cinnamon
⅛ tsp. salt
⅛ tsp. pepper
1 tsp. chopped fresh chives
fresh rosemary sprigs for garnish

Parboil potatoes for 10 minutes and drain. Sprinkle with paprika. Heat olive oil in a skillet over medium heat. Add onion and rosemary and sauté for 5 minutes. Add potatoes; sprinkle with cinnamon, salt and pepper. Flip potatoes over occasionally and cook until golden brown and tender. Transfer potatoes to a serving bowl. Top with fresh chives and garnish with a sprig of fresh rosemary.

GREEN BEAN AND MUSHROOM SAUTÉ

Servings: 4-6

For best results, look for pencil-thin green or yellow snap beans for quick sautés. For a variation, you can toss with other herbs including mint, basil, dill or chives.

1 lb. fresh green or yellow snap beans,
  washed and ends removed
1 tbs. butter
1 tbs. olive or canola oil
2 tbs. finely chopped shallots
½ lb. mushrooms, sliced
2 tsp. fresh lemon juice
1 tsp. chopped fresh parsley, or ¼ tsp.
  dried

⅛ tsp. dried rosemary
½ tsp. garlic powder
⅛ tsp. salt
¼ tsp. pepper
1 tsp. grated Parmesan cheese, optional

Chop beans diagonally into ½-inch pieces. Melt butter and heat oil in a large skillet over medium heat. Add shallots and sauté for 2 minutes. Add beans and sauté for 3 more minutes or until tender but still crisp. Add mushroom slices and lemon juice. Reduce heat to low and sauté for 8 to 10 minutes or until mushrooms are cooked. Transfer to a serving bowl and toss with fresh parsley, rosemary, garlic powder, salt and pepper. Top with a sprinkle of grated Parmesan cheese if desired. Serve warm.

TOMATO SAUTÉ BRUSCHETTE

Servings: 2

We like to serve this warm, but it's traditionally served chilled. The choice is yours — it's delicious either way.

1 French loaf, about 7 inches
1 tbs. olive oil
1 clove garlic, minced
4 thin slices prociutto
1 can (2.25 oz.) sliced black olives, drained
5 fresh plum tomatoes, cut into 1-inch chunks
1 tbs. balsamic vinegar
1 tbs. chopped fresh basil

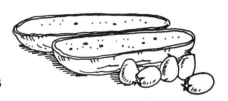

Cut bread in half lengthwise. Toast bread under the boiler until golden brown and set aside. Heat oil in a skillet over medium heat. Add garlic and sauté for 1 minute. Add prosciutto and olives; sauté for 1 more minute. Add tomatoes and vinegar and sauté until warm, about 1½ minutes. Spread mixture evenly over toasted bread. Sprinkle with basil and serve.

VARIATION
Replace tomato chunks with 1-inch zucchini slices cut into quarters.

VEGETABLE GARDENER'S DELIGHT

Servings: 4

Crunchy, colorful sautéed fresh vegetables and walnuts — a winning combination good with any entrée.

1 lb. green or yellow snap beans, about
  3 cups
water
1 tbs. olive or canola oil
1 red bell pepper, sliced into matchstick
  strips

1 medium carrot, peeled and cut into
  matchstick strips
2 cloves garlic, minced or pressed
½ cup coarsely chopped walnuts
salt and pepper to taste

Remove bean ends and slice into 2-inch pieces. Bring 1 inch of water to a boil in a 10- or 12-inch skillet. Add beans and boil for 5 minutes or until just cooked and still crisp. Drain beans and discard water. Heat oil in skillet. Add bell pepper, carrot and garlic. Sauté for 3 minutes over medium heat. Add beans and walnuts. Sauté for 2 minutes. Transfer to a serving bowl, season with salt and pepper and serve warm or chilled.

VARIATION
Substitute almond slivers for the chopped walnuts.

CRISPY HERB CROUTONS

Yield: 3 cups

Homemade crispy croutons will liven up any garden salad. It's a clever way to use up day-old bread. And they go well with hot and cold soups as well. You can keep the butter and oil at a minimum if you use a nonstick skillet.

3 slices day-old bread, 1/2-3/4-inch thick
2 tbs. butter
2 tbs. canola or olive oil
1/2 tsp. dried basil
1/2 tsp. dried oregano
1/4 tsp. garlic powder

Evenly cut bread slices into 1-inch cubes. Do not remove crusts. Melt butter with oil in a skillet over medium-high heat. Add bread cubes. Sprinkle with basil, oregano and garlic powder. Stir continuously for about 8 to 10 minutes or until crisp and evenly browned. Remove from pan. Let cool and serve, or store in an airtight container.

SAUTÉED SESAME BROCCOLI AND GREENS

Servings: 4

We like to cook this with equal amounts of broccoli and cauliflower, but it can be prepared with 6 cups of either. For variety, substitute collard greens, broccoli de rabe or turnip greens for the mustard greens.

1½ cups broccoli florets and sliced stems
1½ cups cauliflower florets and sliced stems
1 tbs. canola oil
1 clove garlic, minced or pressed
½ lb. fresh mustard greens, coarsely chopped
½ tbs. light soy sauce
½ tsp. sesame seeds, toasted
4 drops sesame oil

Steam or parboil broccoli and cauliflower for 2 to 3 minutes. Drain and set aside. Heat oil in a large skillet over medium-high heat. Add garlic and sauté for 1 minute. Add mustard greens; stir occasionally until limp, about 4 to 5 minutes. Add broccoli and cauliflower; stir in soy sauce and sesame seeds. Sauté for 4 to 5 minutes or until broccoli is cooked but tender. Transfer to a serving bowl and toss with sesame oil.

SAUTÉED VEGETABLE GREENS AND APPLE

Servings: 4

Use any fresh vegetable greens in this recipe: kale, collard greens, mustard greens, turnip greens or broccoli de rabe.

6 cups vegetable greens
1 tbs. butter
2 tbs. canola or olive oil
1 medium onion, chopped
1 Granny Smith apple, peeled, cored
  and chopped
$1/8$ tsp. salt

$1/8$ tsp. pepper
$1/4$ tsp. dried basil
1 tbs. balsamic vinegar
1 tbs. fresh lemon juice
1 tbs. pine nuts

Prepare greens by washing, cutting off tough stems and trimming large veins. Melt butter with 1 tbs. of the oil in a skillet over medium heat. Stir in prepared greens. Coat thoroughly with butter-oil mixture; cover and cook for 7 to 12 minutes. Remove greens from skillet and set aside. Heat remaining 1 tbs. oil in skillet. Add onion and sauté for 3 to 4 minutes. Add apple and sauté for 2 to 3 minutes. Stir in greens. Sprinkle with salt, pepper and basil. Drizzle with vinegar and lemon juice. Add pine nuts and sauté for 1 minute. Transfer to a serving bowl. Serve warm.

SWEET APPLE AND PEAR SAUTÉ

We especially like to serve this side dish with pork.

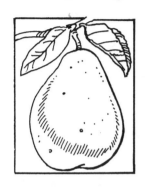

1 large apple, Cortland, Baldwin or Granny Smith
1 large pear, Bartlett or Bosc
1 tbs. butter
1 tbs. canola oil
1 medium Vidalia onion, diced
1 stalk celery, thinly sliced
$\frac{1}{4}$ cup "lite" maple syrup
1 tbs. finely chopped walnuts

Peel and remove cores from apple and pear and slice into wedges. Melt butter and heat oil in a skillet over medium heat. Add onion and celery and sauté for 4 to 5 minutes. Add apple and pear wedges and sauté for 6 to 8 minutes. Reduce heat to low and stir in maple syrup and walnuts. Serve warm.

SAUTÉED BRUSSELS SPROUTS WITH GARLIC AND CASHEWS

Servings: 4

This lavish treatment is good with almost any sautéed vegetable.

2 tbs. olive oil
4 cloves garlic, sliced
$1/8$ tsp. red pepper flakes, optional
1 lb. Brussels sprouts, cut into quarters
$1/4$ cup unsalted roasted cashews

Heat oil in a skillet. Add garlic slices and pepper flakes; sauté over medium heat for 2 minutes or until lightly golden brown. Add Brussels sprouts and sauté for 5 to 7 minutes. Transfer to a serving bowl and toss with roasted cashews.

VARIATION
Substitute broccoli or artichoke hearts for Brussels sprouts.

VEGETABLE FRITTATA

You can serve this as the main course at an informal dinner, or slice it into small wedges and let it be part of an antipasto, with lots of fresh Italian breads, red and green grapes and a bottle of wine. For best results, use room-temperature eggs for a nice large volume and smooth texture. Flip the frittata over with 2 large spatulas or a flat dish.

½ lb. zucchini
3 tbs. flour
2 tbs. butter
2 tbs. olive oil
¼ lb. mushrooms, sliced
1 small onion, minced
4 eggs
2 tbs. grated Parmesan or Romano cheese
½ tsp. dried basil
⅛ tsp. salt
¼ tsp. pepper
⅓ tsp. dried parsley, or 1 tsp. chopped fresh

Slice zucchini into 1/4-inch rounds. Dredge zucchini rounds in flour. Melt 1 tbs. of the butter with oil in a 10-inch skillet over medium-high heat. As soon as butter starts to bubble, cook zucchini rounds over medium-high heat on both sides until lightly golden brown. Remove cooked zucchini from pan and set aside. Melt remaining 1 tbs. butter in skillet and add mushrooms and onion. Cover pan; cook over medium-low heat until onion is tender. Stir occasionally. In a medium bowl, beat eggs and combine with cheese, basil, salt and pepper. Scatter zucchini rounds in skillet and mix with mushrooms and onion. Pour in egg mixture. Cover and cook over low heat for 15 to 18 minutes or until bottom of frittata is firm and golden brown. Turn frittata over, cover and cook for 10 more minutes. Transfer frittata to a large serving platter and sprinkle with parsley. Serve hot, or refrigerate and serve cold.

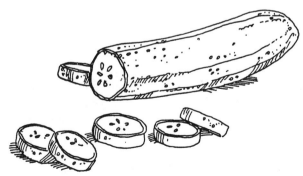

HEARTY QUESADILLAS WITH FRESH SALSA
Servings: 2

These quesadillas are a perfect accompaniment to a salad or a bowl of soup for lunch, and make a tempting appetizer or snack on their own.

1/2 cup refried beans
1 roasted garlic bulb, directions follow
1 tsp. minced fresh cilantro
1/8 tsp. pepper
4 large flour tortillas

1 can (2.25 oz.) sliced black olives
2 small jalapeño peppers, diced
2 medium tomatoes, diced
1 cup shredded cheddar cheese
Fresh Salsa, follows

In a small bowl, combine beans, garlic, cilantro and pepper. Mash together. Spread a thin layer of bean mixture on half of each tortilla. Top mixture with olives, jalapeños, tomatoes and cheese. Fold over other half. Place in a nonstick preheated dry skillet over medium-high heat. Cook until all ingredients are heated through, about 4 minutes on each side. Cut each quesadilla in half and serve with *Fresh Salsa*.

FRESH SALSA
Yield: about 2 cups

2 cups diced plum tomatoes
2 tbs. minced fresh cilantro
2 tbs. chopped jalapeño peppers
1/3 cup chopped red onion
1/2 cup chopped red bell pepper

1/2 cup chopped cucumber
1 tbs. fresh lemon juice
1 tsp. fresh lime juice
1 tsp. chili powder

In a food processor or blender, combine all ingredients and blend until pureed, or leave somewhat chunky, as desired. Refrigerate for at least 3 hours before serving.

ROASTED GARLIC

Garlic that has been roasted takes on a much milder and sweeter flavor than raw garlic. Use fresh bulbs with a firm texture and no signs of sprouting. Use roasted garlic in recipes, or as a spread on crusty bread. A garlic baker works well, but you will get satisfactory results if you wrap the bulb in foil.

1 large bulb garlic	1/8 tsp. dried basil
1/4 tsp. or 1 tbs. olive oil (see method)	1/8 tsp. dried thyme
1 tsp. butter, optional	freshly ground pepper to taste

For perfectly roasted garlic, cut 1/4-inch off top of garlic bulb. Remove loose outer leaves. Bulb should remain intact. Pour 1/4 tsp. olive oil over bulb and dot with butter, or pour 1 tbs. olive oil over bulb and eliminate butter. Sprinkle with basil, thyme and pepper. Place cover on garlic baker or wrap in foil. For a medium to large bulb, bake in a preheated 350° oven for 50 minutes. For a very large bulb, bake for an additional 10 minutes. If cooking in a microwave oven, prepare bulb, place in garlic baker or other covered microwavable container (not foil) and cook on HIGH for 1 1/2 minutes. Separate cloves and squeeze out garlic.

MIXED VEGETABLE TACOS

Servings: 4

Indulge in these spicy and creative tacos. Serve two per person for a great meal.

1 jalapeño pepper
1 large red, green or yellow bell pepper, cut into 1/4-inch strips
1 medium onion, thinly sliced
1 summer squash (zucchini, yellow crookneck or pattypan) cut into
  1/4-x-3-inch strips
4 cups thinly sliced white mushrooms
1/2 cup water
1/2 tsp. chili powder
1/4 tsp. ground cumin
1/4 tsp. paprika
1/4 tsp. dry mustard
dash cayenne pepper
8 large flour or whole wheat tortillas
1/2 cup shredded cheddar cheese
1 1/2 cups shredded fresh spinach
3/4 cup diced tomatoes
sour cream, optional

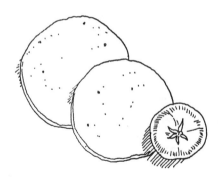

Roast jalapeño pepper: slice pepper in half lengthwise. Remove all seeds and ribs. Place pepper halves skin side up under the oven broiler. Broil for 10 minutes or until skins are blistered and charred. Place peppers in a plastic or paper bag and let sweat for 10 minutes. Remove peppers from bag, peel off skins and chop into small pieces.

In a large nonstick skillet over medium-high heat, sauté peppers, onion, squash and mushrooms for 5 to 6 minutes; stir frequently. Add water and all spices. Bring to a quick boil and remove from heat. Heat tortillas according to package instructions. Spread equal amounts of vegetable mixture in center of each tortilla. Top with shredded cheese, spinach and tomatoes. Fold both edges of each tortilla over so they overlap in the center. Pinch edges to hold shape and serve immediately. Serve with sour cream if desired.

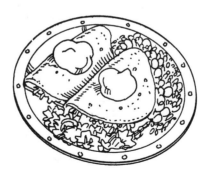

CHEESE AND HERB OMELET

Serving: 1

It's a good idea to let the eggs sit at room temperature for a few minutes since very cold eggs will reduce the temperature of the skillet, resulting in a slow cooked and disappointing omelet. For best results, quickly cook your omelets one at a time with only 2 or 3 eggs in a 7- or 8-inch skillet. With a little practice and patience, anyone can easily master the art of preparing perfect omelets.

2 large or 3 medium eggs
1 tbs. fresh chopped parsley, dill, chervil,
  thyme, tarragon or chives, or 1 tsp. dried
salt and pepper to taste

2 tsp. butter or margarine
3 tbs. shredded cheddar, Swiss,
  Gruyère or Jarlsberg cheese

Remove eggs from the refrigerator for 10 minutes. In a medium bowl, beat eggs with a wire whisk with herbs, salt and pepper. Melt butter in a skillet over medium heat. As soon as butter starts foaming but before it browns, quickly pour in eggs. Wait just a few seconds. With a fork, gently lift edges of eggs, tipping skillet to let uncooked egg run directly onto skillet surface. Repeat around entire omelet, 12 to 16 seconds. Eggs should be cooked on bottom and top will be moist and a little runny. Spread cheese across center of omelet. With a wide, thin spatula, fold ⅓ of the omelet over the center. Slide omelet out of pan onto a warm serving plate. Fold remaining ⅓ over center of omelet as it flips out of pan. Serve immediately.

SAUTÉS FOR PASTA AND PIZZA

VEGETABLE AND FETA MEDLEY WITH PASTA

Servings: 4

Here's a pretty dish to add to your repertoire. Serve it in individual bowls or on a large platter. It's perfect for buffets or family-style dinners. The recipe calls for a small jar of roasted peppers, but you can very easily and economically prepare your own roasted peppers by following the directions on page 93.

1 pkg. (16 oz.) dried pasta, ziti or spaghetti, broken into thirds
2 tbs. olive oil
2 cloves garlic, minced or pressed
1/4 cup water
4 cups fresh spinach
2 large tomatoes, cut into 1-inch chunks

1 jar (7.5 oz.) roasted peppers, drained and diced
1/4 cup crumbled feta cheese
1/2 tsp. dried oregano, or 1 1/2 tsp. fresh
1/2 tsp. dried basil, or 1 1/2 tsp. fresh
pinch salt
1/8 tsp. pepper

Cook pasta according to package instructions. While pasta is cooking, heat oil in a nonstick or stick-resistant skillet over medium heat. Add garlic and sauté for 2 to 3 minutes or until light golden brown. Add water and spinach. Cook until all spinach is wilted. Add tomatoes and cook until just warmed through, about 3 to 4 minutes. Remove skillet from heat. Drain pasta. In a large bowl, toss pasta with roasted peppers, feta cheese, herbs, salt and pepper. Pour tomato-spinach mixture and all liquid from skillet over pasta. Mix well and serve warm or chilled.

ROASTED BELL PEPPERS   Servings: 2-4

When preparing roasted peppers, it's a good idea to remove the seeds and ribs before roasting. Roasted peppers are easy to prepare and a popular ingredient in many sautés. Serve as a side dish or over toasted slices of French bread topped with black olive slices.

4 large red or yellow bell peppers

Slice peppers in half and remove all seeds and ribs. Preheat the broiler. Place pepper halves on a baking sheet with the skin side up. Gently flatten peppers and cook under hot broiler for 10 to 12 minutes, turning occasionally, until peppers are blistered and charred. Place peppers in a plastic or paper bag. Seal and let peppers sweat for 10 minutes. Peel off and discard skins. Slice peppers into strips and set aside for use in recipes or toss roasted pepper strips in a bowl with olive oil, garlic powder, salt and pepper. Refrigerate for at least 30 minutes before serving.

NORTH END-STYLE PASTA

Sample a taste of Boston's North End. This recipe may sound simple, but once you taste this combination of olive oil and herbs you may never go back to a red sauce again. Just don't skimp on the quality. Use extra virgin olive oil, fresh herbs and the best quality Parmesan cheese you can find. Serve as a side dish to veal or chicken. Or serve with hot garlic bread and a fresh vegetable salad and you have created a full course Italian-style meal. Don't forget the vino!

⅔ cup extra virgin olive oil
8 cloves garlic, minced or pressed
1 pkg. (16 oz.) dried spaghetti or angel
  hair pasta
1 cup chicken broth
¾ cup chopped fresh basil

2 tbs. chopped fresh parsley
¼ tsp. pepper
fresh basil or parsley sprigs for garnish,
  optional
freshly grated Parmesan cheese

Heat oil in a small skillet over medium-low heat. Add garlic and sauté for a few minutes or until lightly golden brown. Stir frequently and do not overcook. Cook pasta according to package instructions. Drain and return pasta to empty saucepan. Add chicken broth to pasta and heat over medium-low heat. Add garlic-oil mixture. Stir in basil, parsley and pepper. Stir frequently until well mixed and heated. Transfer to a large platter or individual serving plates. Garnish with fresh basil or parsley sprigs if desired. Top with a generous sprinkle of Parmesan cheese.

EGGPLANT RATATOUILLE

Servings: 2

We prefer this dish with fresh herbs, but you can substitute dried, just use one-third the quantity. It's also delicious served in individual soup bowls or over brown rice.

1 pkg. (8 oz.) dried large bow tie pasta
3 tbs. olive oil plus 1 tsp. olive oil
2 cloves garlic, minced or pressed
1 small onion, finely chopped
1 medium eggplant, peeled and cut
  into 1-inch cubes
1 medium red bell pepper
1 medium green bell pepper
1/2 medium zucchini

1/2 medium yellow crookneck squash
1 can (14 oz.) stewed tomatoes with
  juice, or 5 plum tomatoes, diced
1/4 tsp. red pepper flakes
1 tsp. chopped fresh basil
1 tsp. chopped fresh parsley
1 tsp. chopped fresh oregano
1/4 tsp. pepper

Cook pasta according to package instructions. Drain, toss with 1 tsp. of the olive oil and set aside. While pasta is cooking, heat remaining 3 tbs. oil in a skillet over medium-high heat. Sauté garlic and onion for 2 to 3 minutes. Add all remaining ingredients except spices and herbs. Reduce heat to medium-low and cook for 15 to 20 minutes or until vegetables are cooked through. Add spices and herbs. Stir thoroughly and serve over bow tie pasta on individual serving plates or a large platter.

ANGEL HAIR PASTA WITH SUMMER VEGETABLES

Servings: 4

This eye-appealing dish is as delicious as it is beautiful. The secret to the great flavor is the fresh basil and tomatoes. Serve with hot Italian rolls.

12 oz. dried angel hair pasta
1 tsp. plus 2 tbs. olive oil
2 cloves garlic, minced or pressed
½ cup chopped onion
1 bell pepper, red, green or yellow, cut into 1-inch pieces
1 medium yellow crookneck squash, cut into 1-inch slices, quartered
1 medium zucchini, cut into 1-inch slices, quartered
2 tbs. chopped scallions
¼ cup finely chopped celery
1 cup peeled eggplant cubes, ½-inch
¼ tsp. dried thyme
¼ tsp. pepper
3 cups plum tomatoes, cut into small chunks
¼ cup chicken broth
2 tbs. chopped fresh basil
freshly grated Romano or Parmesan cheese

Cook angel hair pasta according to package instructions. Drain well, toss with 1 tsp. oil and set aside. While pasta is cooking, heat 2 tbs. olive oil in a large nonstick skillet over medium heat. Add garlic and onion; sauté for 2 minutes. Add bell pepper, yellow crookneck squash, zucchini, scallions, celery, eggplant, thyme and pepper. Sauté for 7 to 8 minutes. Add tomatoes and chicken broth. Reduce heat to low. Cover skillet and sauté for 5 minutes or until tomatoes are heated through. Stir occasionally. Remove from heat and stir in fresh basil. Distribute cooked pasta on 4 warm serving plates. Carefully spoon tomato mixture, with all remaining liquid, over pasta. Sprinkle with freshly grated cheese.

FRESH SPINACH AND PASTA SAUTÉ

Here's proof that you don't need a long list of ingredients to create a pleasing meal. A vegetarian's delight — very low on fat. Do not substitute frozen spinach.

16 oz. dried ziti or penne pasta
1 tbs. pine nuts, optional
2½ cups water
3 chicken bouillon cubes
1½ tbs. flour
10 oz. fresh spinach, torn
freshly grated Parmesan cheese

Cook pasta according to package instructions. Drain and set aside. Place pine nuts in a dry nonstick skillet. Stir constantly over low heat for 1 to 2 minutes or until nuts turn golden brown. Bring water to a boil in a 10- or 12-inch skillet. Add bouillon cubes. When bouillon cubes dissolve, reduce heat setting to medium-low and slowly whisk in flour. Add spinach and stir frequently until spinach has cooked down. Add cooked pasta to spinach mixture. Stir thoroughly and heat over medium-low heat for 3 to 4 minutes. Transfer to a large serving platter or individual serving plates. Top with roasted pine nuts. Serve with freshly grated Parmesan cheese.

SAVORY CHICKEN AND RAVIOLI

Servings: 2

You'll agree that this is a truly outstanding and delicious dish with a dazzling presentation. It's perfect with a garden salad.

2 chicken breast halves, skinned and boned
1 pkg. (18 oz.) fresh or frozen cheese-filled ravioli
2 tsp. plus 1 tbs. olive oil
1 clove garlic, minced or pressed
¾ lb. mushrooms, thinly sliced
6 fresh plum tomatoes, cut into 1-inch chunks
2 tbs. balsamic vinegar
1 tbs. chopped fresh basil

Rinse chicken and pat dry. Cut chicken into ½-inch strips. Cook ravioli according to package instructions. Drain, toss with 2 tsp. olive oil and set aside. While ravioli is cooking, heat 1 tbs. oil in a skillet over medium-high heat. Add garlic and sauté for 1 minute. Add chicken strips and sauté for 2 to 3 minutes. Add mushrooms and sauté for 5 minutes. Add plum tomatoes and vinegar; sauté until tomatoes are heated through. Distribute cooked ravioli on 4 individual serving plates. Cover ravioli with equal portions of chicken mixture. Top with fresh basil and serve immediately.

SKILLET-ROASTED SQUASH
WITH CHICKEN AND RIGATONI

Servings: 4-6

Serve this special pasta salad as a side dish or a nutritious lunch entrée. You can combine the rigatoni with other pastas including tortellini, ziti, penne or rotelle.

16 oz. dried rigatoni (tubes with ridges)
1 tbs. pine nuts
1 small zucchini, cut into ½-x-2½-inch strips
1 small yellow crookneck squash, cut into ½-x-2½-inch strips
1 tsp. canola oil
2 oz. fresh snow pea pods
2 chicken breast halves, skinned, boned and cooked
1 radish, thinly sliced
1 large tomato, cut into large chunks
1 tsp. chopped fresh mint
¾ cup *Herb Dressing*, follows

Cook pasta according to package directions. Rinse under cold water and drain well. Set aside. Place pine nuts in a dry skillet and heat over medium-low heat for 1 to 2 minutes or until nuts are lightly brown. Remove from skillet and set aside. Heat a dry nonstick skillet or stick-resistant skillet over medium-high heat for 2 minutes. Place squash strips in skillet, 6 to 8 pieces at a time, and cook for 3 to 4 minutes. Stir frequently. Remove cooked squash and set aside. Repeat process until all squash is cooked. Heat oil in skillet over medium-high heat. Add pea pods, stir frequently and cook for 20 seconds or until pea pods turn a darker shade of green. Remove from skillet and set aside. Slice cooked chicken breasts into 1½-x-3-inch strips. In a large bowl, combine pasta, squash, chicken strips, radish slices, pea pods, tomatoes, mint and pine nuts. Add *Herb Dressing* and toss well. Cover and refrigerate for at least 2 hours. Serve chilled.

HERB DRESSING
Yield: ¾ cup

You'll like this over over cold pasta or fresh vegetable salads.

3 tbs. olive oil
¼ cup water
6 tbs. balsamic vinegar
2 cloves garlic, minced or pressed
½ tsp. dried basil

¼ tsp. dried oregano
¼ tsp. dried marjoram
½ tsp. dried thyme
⅛ tsp. salt
¼ tsp. pepper

Combine all ingredients in a medium bowl and whisk until blended.

SAUTÉED CHICKEN SAUSAGE WITH FRESH SAGE

Here's a pasta dish with a new twist to an Italian tradition. This is a great way to use chicken sausage. Serve with fresh hot rolls or Italian bread slices.

2 cups dried ziti, rigatoni, cavatelli or
  penne pasta
1 tsp. plus 1 tbs. olive or canola oil
½ lb. chicken or turkey sausage
1 tbs. butter
2 cups chicken broth

2 tbs. cornstarch
4 cups coarsely chopped Swiss chard or
  ruby red Swiss chard
1 tbs. chopped fresh sage
¼ tsp. pepper
2 tbs. shredded Jarlsberg cheese

Cook pasta according to package instructions. Drain, toss with 1 tsp. oil and set aside. While pasta is cooking, prepare topping. Cut sausage into ½-inch round slices. Melt butter with 1 tbs. oil in a skillet over medium heat. Add sausage and brown on all sides for 4 to 6 minutes. Remove sausage from pan and set aside. Pour chicken broth into skillet and heat over medium heat. Whisk in cornstarch. Add Swiss chard and cook for 4 to 5 minutes. Return sausage to skillet; add fresh sage and pepper. Mix well. Stir in cheese until blended. Remove from heat and combine with pasta in a large bowl or in 2 individual serving bowls. Serve immediately.

SHRIMP FETTUCCINE

This is one of the easiest and best preparations for shrimp. Serve this with a hot crusty loaf of bread and a fresh vegetable salad.

1 lb. large shrimp
6 oz. dried fettuccine
3 tbs. butter
3 tbs. olive oil
1/3 cup finely chopped red onion
3 cloves garlic, minced or pressed
2 tsp. chopped fresh basil

1 tsp. chopped fresh thyme
2 tsp. chopped fresh oregano
1/2 cup white wine
4 lemon wedges for garnish
1 tsp. chopped fresh parsley for garnish
freshly grated Parmesan cheese

Peel and devein shrimp. Wash and pat dry. Cook fettuccine according to package instructions. While pasta is cooking, melt butter with oil in a skillet over medium-high heat. Add onion and garlic and sauté for 3 minutes. Add basil, thyme, oregano and shrimp. Stir and cook for 2 minutes. Pour in wine; stir and cook for 2 more minutes. Drain fettuccine. Serve shrimp mixture over fettuccine on 2 individual serving plates. Garnish with lemon wedges and a sprinkle of fresh parsley. Serve with freshly grated Parmesan cheese.

SPICY HERB SCALLOPS OVER ANGEL HAIR PASTA

This dish tastes equally delicious over most other pastas including linguine, spaghetti, fettuccine, bow ties or penne. It's nice to serve at a special dinner party. Use your favorite tomato sauce, or our recipe on page 33.

1 lb. whole bay scallops, or sea scallops, cut into thirds
1 tbs. olive oil
4 cloves garlic, minced or pressed
3 large shallots, chopped
3 cups tomato sauce
¾ cup chopped mushrooms
2 tbs. chopped sun-dried tomatoes, packed in oil or reconstituted

¼ tsp. dried oregano
¼ tsp. dried thyme
¼ tsp. dried basil
¼ tsp. red pepper flakes
1 pkg. (16 oz.) dried angel hair pasta
1 cup chopped fresh spinach
1 tbs. chopped fresh parsley
freshly grated Parmesan cheese

Rinse scallops. To release liquid from scallops, place in a dry nonstick skillet set on low heat. Raise heat setting to medium and cook for 2 minutes. Remove scallops from pan and drain. Heat oil in a deep straight-sided sauté pan (2- to 4-quart) over medium heat and sauté garlic and shallots for 2 minutes. Add tomato sauce, mushrooms, sun-dried tomatoes, oregano, thyme, basil and pepper flakes. Stir thoroughly. Cover pan and simmer for 15 minutes. While sauce simmers, cook pasta according to package instructions. Stir scallops and spinach into sauce. Cover and cook over medium heat for 5 to 6 minutes or until scallops are just cooked through. Drain pasta, divide onto 4 warm serving plates and top with equal portions of tomato-scallop mixture. Sprinkle with fresh parsley and serve with freshly grated Parmesan cheese.

VARIATION
Substitute chunks of cooked artichoke hearts for the spinach.

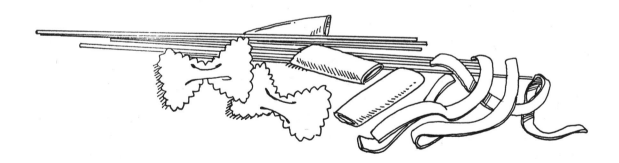

SAUSAGE AND TORTELLINI SAUTÉ

Servings: 4

Fresh fennel, lentils and sausage come together beautifully. This is a superb attraction to headline your next buffet table.

½ cup lentils
1 tbs. olive oil
1 lb. Italian sausage, cut into 1-inch
   pieces
1 fennel bulb, cut into 1-inch pieces
¼ tsp. pepper

1 small onion, minced
1 cup tomato juice
½ tsp. dried basil
1 pkg. (14 oz.) cheese tortellini, fresh or
   frozen
2 tbs. chopped scallions

Rinse lentils under cold water. Bring lentils to a boil in water, reduce heat and simmer for 40 minutes. Drain and set aside. Heat oil in a skillet over medium-high heat. Add sausage and sauté until golden brown on each side, about 5 minutes. Remove sausage from pan and set aside. Reduce heat to medium, place fennel, pepper and onions in pan and sauté for 10 minutes. Add tomato juice, basil, lentils and sausage to pan; cover and simmer for 13 to 15 minutes. While mixture simmers, cook tortellini according to package instructions. Drain tortellini and combine in a large bowl with all other ingredients. Mix well and serve on individual serving plates. Sprinkle with chopped scallions.

LIGHT AND EASY TURKEY PASTA SALAD

Servings: 4

For more than 17 years Dave co-owned Kitchen Korner, a specialty kitchenware shop in Massachusetts, with his long-time partner Ellie Fishbein. She and her husband, Bobby, have been willing, brave and loyal recipe tasters. This is one of their favorites, which they strongly recommend.

1 pkg. (8 oz.) dried linguine or angel hair
  pasta
1/3 cup light soy sauce
1 tbs. honey
1 tbs. olive or canola oil
1 lb. turkey breast cutlets, cut into
  1/2-inch strips
1 clove garlic, minced

1 red bell pepper, cut into 1/4-inch strips
1 cup chopped scallions
1 medium zucchini, cut into matchstick
  strips
1 medium carrot, cut into matchstick
  strips
1/2 tsp. grated ginger root
fresh parsley sprigs for garnish

Cook pasta according to package instructions. While pasta is cooking, combine soy sauce with honey in a small bowl and set aside. Heat oil in a large sauté pan over medium-high heat. Add turkey and sauté for 3 to 4 minutes. Add garlic, pepper, scallions, zucchini, carrot and ginger root. Sauté for 3 minutes or until vegetables are tender-crisp. Add soy sauce and honey mixture and stir until hot. Drain pasta, transfer to a large bowl and combine with turkey mixture. Mix well and serve hot on individual serving plates. Garnish with fresh parsley sprigs.

CARAMELIZED ONION AND MUSHROOM PIZZA

Servings: 2
8-10 as appetizer

Let's have pizza! And the best pizza is always homemade. Just be sure to use the freshest and best quality ingredients you can find.

Basic Pizza Dough, page 110, or your
  favorite
3 tbs. olive oil, extra virgin preferably
2 cloves garlic, minced or pressed
½ cup *Caramelized Onions*, follows
5 plum tomatoes, cut into 1-inch chunks
¾ lb. Portobello mushrooms, thinly
  sliced and quartered
⅛ tsp. salt

⅛ tsp. pepper
1 cup tomato sauce, see page 33, or
  your favorite
½ tsp. dried basil
¼ tsp. dried oregano
1¼ cups shredded mozzarella cheese
3 tbs. grated Parmesan cheese
10-15 small fresh basil leaves, or 3 tbs.
  chopped

Prepare pizza dough. Heat 2 tbs. of the oil in a 10-inch skillet over low heat. Add garlic and sauté for 1 to 2 minutes or until garlic is light brown. Add onions, tomatoes, mushrooms, salt and pepper. Sauté over medium heat for 5 minutes. Roll out pizza dough to fit a 14-inch pizza pan, lightly oiled, or a ceramic baking stone, sprinkled with cornmeal. Brush raw dough with remaining 1 tbs. olive oil. Cover pizza dough with tomato-mushroom mixture, leaving a ½-inch border around the edge. Spoon tomato sauce over topping. Sprinkle with dried basil, oregano, mozzarella and Parmesan cheeses. Top with fresh basil leaves. Bake in a preheated 425° oven for 25 to 30 minutes, or until cheese starts to bubble and turn golden brown.

CARAMELIZED ONIONS
Yield: ½ cup

Any of the yellow variety of onions including Vidalia, Grano and Granex will sauté beautifully for making caramelized onions. They have a natural sweet taste that transforms to a spectacular flavor. Serve as pizza toppings or over lamb, beef or pork. Caramelized onions are also delicious with grilled sausage and peppers.

3 tbs. olive or canola oil
2 large or 3 medium yellow onions,
　thinly sliced

1 tbs. balsamic vinegar
salt and pepper to taste
½ tsp. dried thyme

Heat oil in a skillet. Add onions, cover and sauté over medium-low heat for 20 minutes. Stir frequently. Add vinegar, salt, pepper and thyme. Cook uncovered for 5 minutes. Stir frequently until onions are slightly golden brown and caramelized.

BASIC PIZZA DOUGH

Yield: dough for 14-inch pizza

You can also use a bread machine, food processor or heavy-duty mixer to make these doughs.

1 pkg. active dry yeast
1 cup plus 1 tbs. warm water
1 tbs. sugar
3¼ cups all-purpose flour

½ tsp. salt
2 tsp. dried basil
3 tbs. olive oil

In a small bowl, dissolve yeast in water and add sugar. Set aside for 5 minutes. In a large bowl, combine flour, salt and basil and mix well. Add yeast mixture and olive oil to flour mixture. Stir together to form a ball. Place dough on a floured surface and knead for 10 minutes. Place dough in a greased bowl. Cover with a towel or plastic wrap and allow to rise for 1½ hours in a draft-free area. Punch down dough and allow to rest for 10 minutes. Roll out dough to fit a 14-inch pizza pan or ceramic baking stone.

VARIATION: LEMON THYME PIZZA DOUGH

Substitute dried thyme for dried basil, and add 1 clove garlic, minced or pressed and 1 tsp. fresh lemon juice. Proceed as directed.

FESTIVE PIZZA ON A LEMON THYME CRUST

You must try this recipe! It's the perfect topping for a incredible pizza crust. Serve this pizza at your next celebration. Your guests will go wild over it.

Lemon Thyme Pizza Dough, page 110
2 chicken breast halves, skinless and
  boneless
2 tbs. olive oil
2 cloves garlic, minced or pressed
1 lb. mushrooms, halved

2 tbs. chicken broth
4 marinated artichoke hearts, quartered
½ tsp. dried thyme
¼ tsp. pepper
¾ cup freshly grated Parmesan cheese
1 tbs. chopped fresh basil

Prepare dough. Rinse chicken, pat dry and slice into ¼-inch-wide strips. In a large skillet, heat 1 tbs. of the oil over medium heat. Add garlic and sauté for 1 minute. Add mushrooms and chicken broth and sauté for 7 to 8 minutes. Add artichoke hearts, thyme and pepper; sauté for 3 to 4 minutes. Remove from skillet and set aside. Add remaining oil to skillet and heat over medium heat. Add chicken and sauté for 6 to 7 minutes or until chicken is cooked through. Roll out dough to fit a lightly oiled 14-inch pizza pan, or baking stone sprinkled with cornmeal. Spread mushroom-artichoke mixture on dough, leaving a 1-inch border around edge. Top with chicken and sprinkle with Parmesan cheese and basil. Bake in a preheated 425° oven for 25 minutes.

STIR-FRIES

SZECHUAN CHICKEN

Hoisin sauce is a thick, sweet, spicy sauce that's based on soybeans, chile peppers and spices. You'll find it in the Chinese foods section of your supermarket. Szechuan peppercorns can be found in many supermarkets and gourmet shops.

½ cup chicken broth
¼ cup light soy sauce
2 tbs. hoisin sauce
2 tbs. dry sherry
4 chicken breast halves, skinned and
  boned
2 tbs. canola oil
1 tsp. grated ginger root

1 tsp. ground Szechuan peppercorns
1 tbs. brown sugar
½ tsp. anise seeds
1 green or red bell pepper, cut into
  1-inch pieces
½ cup sliced green onions or scallions
1 cup sliced water chestnuts
½ cup unsalted cashews, toasted

In a small bowl, combine broth, soy sauce, hoisin sauce and sherry. Set aside. Rinse chicken and pat dry. Slice chicken into thin strips. Heat oil in a large skillet over high heat. Add ginger root and stir in pepper, brown sugar and anise. Add chicken, bell pepper and scallions. Stir frequently for 5 minutes. Reduce heat to low, add hoisin mixture and cook for 7 minutes. Add chestnuts and cashews and stir. Cook for 2 to 3 more minutes or until hot and chicken is cooked through. Serve on a large platter.

LEMON CHICKEN VEGETABLE STIR-FRY

Servings: 2-4

When stir-frying, use a cooking oil that will not burn or smoke at a high temperature, such as canola, peanut or corn oil. This dish can be prepared in a 10- or 12-inch skillet, a stir-fry pan or a traditional wok.

2 chicken breast halves, skinned and boned
juice of 1/2 lemon
1 clove garlic, minced or pressed
1/2 lb. fresh broccoli
1 red bell pepper
1 medium red onion
1/2 lb. mushrooms
1/2 cup chicken broth
1 tbs. cornstarch
1/2 tsp. grated ginger root
2 tbs. canola oil
cooked white rice
thin lemon slices for garnish

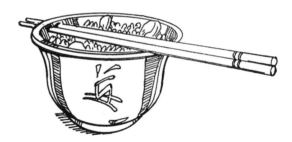

Rinse chicken, pat dry and cut into thin strips, 1-x-2½ inches. In a shallow bowl, combine chicken, lemon juice and garlic. Cover and refrigerate for 45 minutes. Chop broccoli florets into 1-inch pieces and cut stems into matchstick strips. In a medium saucepan, blanch broccoli in boiling water for 1 minute. Plunge broccoli into very cold water; drain and set aside. Cut bell pepper into matchstick strips. Cut red onion into thin slices and separate into rings. Thinly slice mushrooms.

In a small bowl, combine chicken broth, cornstarch and ginger root. Heat 1 tbs. of the oil in a skillet over medium-high heat. Add pepper; stir frequently for 2 minutes. Add mushrooms and continue to stir-fry for 2 more minutes. Add onion and stir-fry for 2 more minutes. Remove to a bowl and set aside. Heat remaining 1 tbs. oil in skillet over medium-high heat. Add chicken with marinade and stir-fry for 3 minutes or until cooked through. Stir in cornstarch mixture. As soon as it starts to bubble, add all vegetables to skillet. Stir-fry for 1 to 2 minutes or until hot. Serve with rice and garnish with lemon slices.

STIR-FRIED CURRY CHICKEN WITH MUSHROOMS

Servings: 2

You can freeze extra chicken broth in an ice cube tray so you'll always have small quantities on reserve. Put the cubes in freezer bags once the broth has frozen. This dish is good over noodles as well as rice.

2 chicken breast halves, skinned and boned
3 tbs. light soy sauce
1 tbs. cornstarch
½ cup chicken broth

1 tbs. canola oil
1 medium onion, chopped
1 tsp. curry powder
1 cup sliced mushrooms
1 stalk celery, thinly sliced

Rinse chicken, pat dry and slice into 1-inch strips. In a shallow bowl, combine soy sauce with chicken. Cover and refrigerate for 30 minutes. In a small bowl, combine cornstarch and chicken broth. Heat oil in a skillet over medium-high heat. Add onion; sprinkle with curry powder and stir-fry for 4 minutes. Place chicken in skillet with all of the soy sauce and stir-fry for 4 minutes. Remove chicken from skillet and set aside. Place mushrooms and celery in skillet and stir-fry for 5 minutes. Add reserved chicken and onions to skillet. Pour in chicken broth mixture. Stir-fry until it boils. Serve immediately.

SESAME CHICKEN WINGS

This popular appetizer recipe can easily be increased. Serve hot or cold.

1 tsp. sesame seeds
1 lb. chicken wings, about 6
1 tbs. light soy sauce
1 clove garlic, minced or pressed
2 tbs. dry sherry
1 tsp. brown sugar
1 tsp. honey

1/4 tsp. red pepper flakes
1 tsp. cornstarch
1/4 tsp. grated ginger root
2 tbs. canola oil
1 small onion, diced
3 tbs. water

Toast sesame seeds in a dry nonstick skillet over medium heat for 30 to 45 seconds or until seeds are lightly golden; stir continuously. Remove from skillet and set aside. Remove excess skin and cut wing tips from chicken wings. Rinse wings and pat dry. In a shallow bowl, combine soy sauce, garlic, sherry, brown sugar, honey, red pepper flakes, cornstarch and ginger root. Mix well. Add chicken wings, coating all sides. Cover and refrigerate for 2 hours or overnight. Heat canola oil in a skillet over medium-high heat. Add onion and cook for 1 minute. Remove chicken wings from bowl, reserving marinade, and place in skillet with onion. Cook for 12 to 15 minutes, stirring frequently. Reduce heat to medium. Add remaining marinade and water. Stir, cover and cook for 10 to 12 minutes. Stir occasionally. Transfer to a small serving platter and sprinkle with toasted sesame seeds.

SWEET AND SOUR SHRIMP

Servings: 2

At first this low fat recipe may sound complicated, but it's actually very simple. Just be prepared to use 3 bowls to prepare the ingredients.

1 lb. large shrimp (about 24), peeled and deveined
1 tbs. light soy sauce
1 tsp. dry sherry
1 cup pineapple chunks
1 tbs. sugar
¾ cup fresh orange juice
½ tsp. fresh lemon juice
½ tsp. fresh lime juice
2 tsp. cornstarch
2 tbs. cider vinegar
1 tbs. plus 2 tsp. canola oil
1 small yellow onion, cut into 1-inch pieces
1 green bell pepper, cut into 1-inch pieces
cooked white rice

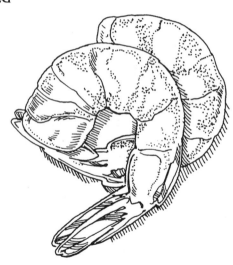

Combine shrimp, soy sauce and sherry in a bowl and set aside. In another bowl, combine pineapple chunks, sugar and all juices. In a small bowl, whisk together cornstarch and vinegar. Heat 2 tsp. of the oil in a skillet over medium-high heat. Add shrimp and stir-fry for 3 to 4 minutes or until shrimp are just pink. Remove shrimp from skillet and set aside. Heat remaining 1 tbs. oil over medium-high heat in skillet. Add onion and pepper and stir-fry until slightly tender. Remove from pan. Over medium-high heat, pour pineapple-cornstarch mixture into pan. Stir constantly. As soon as it bubbles, add onion and pepper. Cook until sauce thickens, about 1 minute. Return shrimp to skillet and stir-fry for 1 more minute. Serve immediately over rice on a large serving platter or on individual serving dishes.

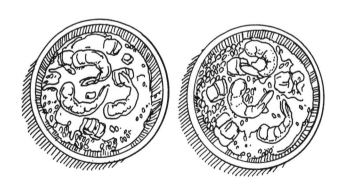

STIR-FRIED SHRIMP WITH LEMON AND FENNEL

Both fresh and frozen shrimp are great for cooking and eating. Both should have a mild ocean scent without even a hint of the smell of ammonia.

1 lb. medium shrimp, about 30-35
1 bunch broccoli, cut into 1-inch pieces
2 tbs. flour
1/8 tsp. paprika
2 tbs. cornmeal
2 tbs. olive or canola oil
2 cloves garlic, minced or pressed
1/8 tsp. salt

2 tbs. fresh lemon juice
1/2 tsp. ground fennel seed
1 large tomato, cut into 1-inch chunks
2 tbs. chopped scallions
cooked white rice
4 lemon wedges
fresh cilantro sprigs for garnish

Peel and devein shrimp. Wash, drain and pat dry. Parboil or steam broccoli for 2 minutes and set aside. In a shallow bowl, mix together flour, paprika and cornmeal. Dredge shrimp in flour mixture. Heat oil in a skillet over medium heat. Add garlic and stir-fry for 1 minute. Stir in salt, lemon juice and fennel seed. Add shrimp and stir-fry for 2 to 3 minutes. Add broccoli and tomatoes and stir-fry for 1 to 1 1/2 minutes. Transfer immediately to 4 serving plates. Sprinkle with chopped scallions. Serve with rice and lemon wedges. Garnish with sprigs of cilantro.

STIR-FRIED CHARRED SHRIMP

Serve these on a platter at your next buffet. Everyone always enjoys great-tasting shrimp.

1½ tbs. butter
1½ tbs. olive or canola oil
1 lb. large shrimp, peeled and deveined,
  tails intact
¼ tsp. dried chervil
¼ tsp. dried marjoram

¾ tsp. curry powder
½ tsp. paprika
2 tsp. grated Parmesan cheese
fresh parsley sprigs for garnish
lemon slices for garnish

Melt butter with oil in a ovenproof skillet over low heat. Add shrimp and stir in chervil, marjoram, curry powder and paprika. Stir-fry for 2 to 3 minutes. Sprinkle shrimp with Parmesan cheese. Place skillet under a preheated broiler for 3 to 4 minutes or until shrimp are lightly charred. Serve on a platter. Garnish with fresh parsley sprigs and lemon slices.

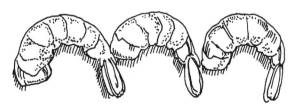

TOMATO CURRY SHRIMP

A picture-pretty dish! The curry adds an interesting spicy flavor to the tomato sauce and blends perfectly with the shrimp. Serve over fresh pasta or rice.

4 cups tomato sauce, your favorite or see page 33
2 tbs. olive or canola oil
1 jalapeño pepper, seeds and ribs removed, finely chopped
1 cup sliced mushrooms
1 tsp. dried coriander
½ tsp. ground cumin
½ tsp. curry powder
1 lb. medium shrimp, shelled and deveined

In a saucepan, heat tomato sauce to a simmer. Heat oil in a skillet over medium heat. Add chopped pepper and stir-fry for 4 minutes. Add mushrooms and stir-fry for 2 more minutes. Stir in coriander, cumin and curry powder. Add shrimp and stir-fry for 2 minutes or until shrimp just turn pink. Stir in tomato sauce and bring to a quick boil. Serve immediately.

RAINBOW SHRIMP

For variety, you can substitute thin slices of white chicken for the shrimp.

½ lb. medium shrimp, shelled and deveined
½ tsp. dry sherry
⅛ tsp. red pepper flakes
1 clove garlic, minced or pressed
½ tsp. cornstarch
2 tbs. unsalted cashews
1½ tbs. canola oil

1 cup pieces fresh pea pods, about 1-inch
1 cup carrot strips, matchstick size
1 tbs. light soy sauce
½ tbs. red wine vinegar
1 cup thinly sliced scallions
½ cup sliced water chestnuts

In a small bowl, combine shrimp, sherry, red pepper flakes, garlic and cornstarch. Mix well and set aside. Heat a skillet over medium-high heat. Add cashews and stir constantly until light golden brown. Remove cashews from skillet and set aside. Heat 1 tbs. of the oil in skillet over medium-high heat. Add shrimp with sherry mixture. Stir-fry for 1 to 2 minutes or until shrimp start to turn pink. Remove shrimp from skillet and set aside. Place pea pods and carrots in skillet and stir-fry for 4 minutes. Add soy sauce, red wine vinegar, remaining ½ tbs. oil, scallions and water chestnuts to skillet. Stir-fry for 3 minutes. Return shrimp to skillet and stir-fry quickly for 1 to 1½ minutes. Sprinkle with cashews and serve immediately.

PORK STIR-FRY

This recipe is for 2 people, or for 3 to 4 as a side dish to a multicourse meal. It has a wonderful refined Chinese flavor with a pleasing display.

½ lb. lean boneless pork
1 tsp. cornstarch
1 tbs. canola oil
1 large onion, chopped
1 tbs. light soy sauce
1 tbs. chopped fresh chives
⅛ tsp. salt
cooked white or brown rice

Cut pork into thin slices. In a small bowl, coat pork strips with cornstarch and set aside. Heat oil in a skillet over high heat. Add onion and stir-fry for 2 minutes. Add pork and stir-fry constantly for 5 more minutes. Add soy sauce, chives and salt. Reduce heat to medium. Stir-fry for 2 more minutes and serve over rice.

ROASTED SESAME PORK AND CABBAGE STIR-FRY

The cabbage adds a sweet, pleasing flavor to the pork. You can successfully store Chinese cabbage in the refrigerator, wrapped in plastic, for 5 days.

2 tbs. sesame seeds
1/2 lb. pork loin, cut into 1-x-2-inch
 pieces
1/4 cup light soy sauce
1 clove garlic, minced or pressed

2 tbs. canola oil
1 lb. Chinese cabbage or bok choy, cut
 into 1/2-inch strips (about 5 cups)
3-4 drops sesame oil
cooked white rice

Toast sesame seeds in a dry nonstick skillet over medium heat, stirring constantly until seeds are golden brown. In a medium bowl, combine pork, sesame seeds, soy sauce and garlic. Cover and marinate in the refrigerator for 2 hours. Heat 1 tbs. of the oil in a large skillet over medium-high heat. Add cabbage. Stir constantly for 3 to 5 minutes or until cabbage leaves wilt. Transfer to a bowl and drain; set aside and keep warm. Heat remaining 1 tbs. canola oil in skillet over medium heat. Add pork mixture and stir-fry for 5 to 6 minutes or until pork is cooked through. Combine pork strips with cabbage and sprinkle with sesame oil. Mix well and serve over rice.

SWEET AND SOUR PORK

Servings: 4-6

You'll love this recipe. Serve it as a dinner for 4, or as the main dish accompanied with steamed or stir-fried vegetables for a larger crowd.

1 lb. boneless pork loin, cut into 1-inch cubes
1 tbs. dry sherry
2 cloves garlic, minced or pressed
½ tsp. grated ginger root
1 can (20 oz.) unsweetened pineapple chunks with juice
1 tbs. light soy sauce
¼ cup water
1 tbs. cornstarch
1 tbs. brown sugar
1 tbs. cider vinegar
1 tsp. red pepper flakes
1 tbs. canola oil
1 cup red bell pepper strips, matchstick size
1 cup green bell pepper strips, matchstick size
½ cup separated thin slices yellow onion
½ cup unsalted cashews, toasted
cooked long-grain rice

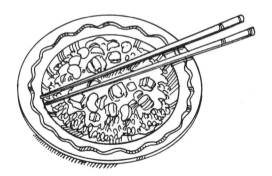

In a shallow bowl, combine pork, sherry, 1 clove garlic and ginger root. Mix well, cover and refrigerate for 45 minutes. In a small bowl, whisk together ¼ cup of the pineapple juice, soy sauce, water, cornstarch, brown sugar, vinegar, remaining 1 clove garlic and red pepper flakes. Set aside. Heat oil in a skillet over medium heat and add pork mixture. Stir-fry for 2 to 3 minutes. Add pineapple-cornstarch sauce and stir thoroughly. Add peppers, onion and pineapple with remaining juice. Cover skillet, reduce heat to low and simmer for 10 minutes. Stir occasionally. Add cashews. Cook for 1 more minute. Serve immediately over rice.

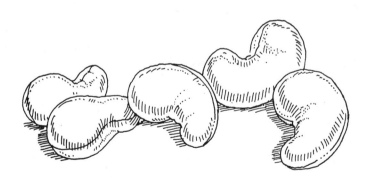

BEEF WITH OYSTER SAUCE

Servings: 4

Oyster sauce is a popular ingredient in a variety of Chinese dishes. It's made from soy sauce and oysters, but doesn't impart a fishy taste.

1 lb. flank or sirloin steak
1 tbs. cornstarch
1 tsp. sugar
½ tsp. dry sherry
2 tbs. low sodium soy sauce
2 tbs. water
1 tsp. grated ginger root
2 tbs. canola oil

1 red or green bell pepper, cut into
  1-inch pieces
1 medium yellow onion, cut into
  1-inch pieces
1 clove garlic, minced or pressed
3 tbs. oyster sauce
cooked white rice

Thinly slice steak into ⅛-inch slices across the grain. In a shallow bowl, combine cornstarch, sugar, sherry, soy sauce, water and ginger root. Mix well; add steak and marinate for 20 minutes. Heat 1 tbs. of the oil in a skillet over high heat. Add pepper and onion and stir-fry for 1 minute. Remove from skillet and set aside. Heat remaining 1 tbs. oil in skillet; add garlic and stir-fry for 30 seconds. Add steak with marinade and stir-fry until cooked through, about 2 minutes. Add oyster sauce. Stir thoroughly and add pepper and onion. Stir-fry until hot and serve immediately with rice.

BEEF AND VEGETABLE CURRY STIR-FRY

Servings: 4

Fresh pea pods blend beautifully with this beef and curry dish. To prepare the pea pods, just snap off the stem end and remove the threads from both seams.

1 lb. flank steak
1 tbs. light soy sauce
1 tbs. sherry
1 tbs. cornstarch
1/4 tsp. sugar
1/8 tsp. salt
2 tbs. canola oil

1 medium onion, thinly sliced
1 tbs. water
1 tbs. curry powder
2 tbs. ketchup
1 1/2 cups pea pod pieces, sliced
  diagonally into thirds
cooked white rice

Trim excess fat from steak. Cut steak into 1/8-x-2 1/2-inch-thick slices across the grain. In a shallow bowl, combine soy sauce, sherry, cornstarch, sugar and salt. Mix well. Add steak to marinade. Cover and refrigerate for 30 minutes. Heat 1 tbs. of the oil in a skillet over high heat. Add onion and stir-fry for 1 minute. Add water, cover and cook for 1 more minute. Remove from pan and transfer to a bowl. Heat remaining 1 tbs. oil in skillet. Stir in curry powder. Add beef and all of the marinade. Stir-fry quickly for about 2 minutes. Add ketchup and stir-fry for 1 more minute. Add onion and pea pods. Stir-fry for 2 to 3 minutes. Transfer to a platter. Serve immediately with rice.

BEEF VEGETABLE DELIGHT

Servings: 2

You can prepare this stir-fry dish and all others in this chapter in a 10- to 14- inch omelet-style skillet with sloping sides, a stir-fry pan or a traditional wok. This pleasing and mildly spicy Chinese dish should be served with lots of steamed long-grain white rice.

½ lb. beef, thinly sliced
2 tbs. light soy sauce
2 tbs. canola oil
1 clove garlic, sliced
1 cup red bell pepper strips, matchstick size

1 cup broccoli pieces, about 1-inch
1 tbs. cider vinegar
1 cup sliced mushrooms
1 cup thinly sliced scallions
¼ cup unsalted peanuts

In a small bowl, combine beef with 1 tbs. of the soy sauce and set aside. Heat 1 tbs. of the oil in a skillet over medium-high heat. Add garlic slices and stir-fry until golden brown. Remove garlic from oil and discard. Place beef with sauce in skillet and stir-fry until cooked through. Remove beef from skillet and set aside. Stir-fry red bell pepper and broccoli for 3 minutes. Add remaining soy sauce, remaining oil and cider vinegar; stir well. Quickly add mushrooms and scallions; stir-fry for 2 minutes. Add beef and peanuts; stir-fry for 1 minute or until beef is hot. Serve immediately.

SPICY BEAN CURD STIR-FRY

Bean curd, also known as tofu, is made from mashed soy beans. It can be found in the refrigerator section in most supermarkets. It's loaded with protein and blends well with most other foods in stir-fry dishes.

¾ lb. bean curd or plain tofu
2 tsp. dry sherry
1 tsp. water
1 tbs. cornstarch
1 tsp. grated ginger root
2 tbs. canola oil

1 clove garlic, minced
¼ lb. shiitake mushrooms, thinly sliced
½ lb. fresh pea pods, about 2½ cups
1 tsp. light soy sauce
1 tsp. sugar
cooked white rice, optional

Cut bean curd into ½-inch cubes. Place cubes on layers of paper towels. Blot with another paper towel to remove excess moisture. In a small bowl, mix together sherry, water, cornstarch and ginger root. Set aside. Heat oil in a skillet over medium-high heat. Add garlic and stir-fry for 1 minute. Add bean curd and stir-fry for 2 to 3 minutes. Add mushrooms, pea pods, soy sauce and sugar. Stir in sherry mixture; stir frequently for 3 to 4 minutes. Serve over rice or in a large serving bowl.

SAUTÉED DESSERTS

FRESH FRUIT SAUTÉ

If fresh raspberries are not in season, you can increase the quantity of strawberries. Serve over shortcakes or slices of angel food cake topped with whipped cream or frozen yogurt. You may also chill the fruit and serve dessert chilled. Also delicious over waffles, pancakes, French toast and any plain white cake or ice cream.

1 medium firm apple
3 cups fresh strawberries
1½ cups fresh blueberries
1 cup fresh raspberries
¼ cup sugar
¼ tsp. cinnamon

Peel, core and slice apple into ¼-inch cubes. Slice strawberries into thick wedges. In a large nonstick skillet, combine blueberries, apple, strawberries, raspberries, sugar and cinnamon. Stir well and cook over medium-low heat for 15 minutes. Remove fruit from pan and serve immediately, or cool and refrigerate before serving.

SUNSHINE FRUIT SALAD

Here's a healthy, light dessert full of flavor and color. Be sure to use a top-quality balsamic vinegar to flavor the fruit.

3 kiwi fruit, peeled, cut into 1/4-inch slices
1 cup strawberry halves
1/2 orange, sectioned
1/2 cup seedless red or green grapes
1 tsp. balsamic vinegar
1/2 cup water
2 tbs. sugar
1 tbs. fresh lemon juice
vanilla cookie chunks, optional

In a medium bowl, combine kiwi, strawberries, orange sections and grapes. Sprinkle with balsamic vinegar and mix well. Heat water in a 8-inch skillet over low heat. Add sugar and lemon juice. Stir continuously until sugar dissolves. Raise heat to medium-high and bring to a quick boil for 2 minutes. Remove skillet from heat and let sauce cool. Pour sauce over fruit and mix carefully. Serve in individual servings bowls and mix in cookie chunks if desired.

STRAWBERRY PUDDING SAUTÉ

You and your guests will love this special treat. It's gorgeous and the flavor is amazing. It may become your favorite dessert.

½ cup flour
¼ cup sugar
1 egg white
2 tbs. butter, melted
¼ tsp. cinnamon
½ tsp. baking powder
1 tbs. apple juice
½ tbs. cornstarch

⅓ cup water
2 tbs. sugar
¼ tsp. cinnamon
2 cups fresh strawberry slices
coconut flakes or chopped almonds
whipped cream
4 fresh mint leaves for garnish

In a medium bowl, combine flour, sugar, egg white, butter, ¼ tsp. cinnamon and baking powder. In a small bowl, whisk together apple juice and cornstarch. Bring water to a boil in a skillet. Add sugar, cinnamon, strawberries and juice mixture. Stir constantly and gently for 1½ minutes or until sauce thickens and reduces. Place dollops of dough over strawberry mixture in skillet. Cover skillet and cook over medium-low heat for 11 minutes. Spoon into individual serving bowls. Top with coconut flakes or almonds and whipped cream. Garnish with mint leaves. Serve immediately.

FRESH BERRY TOPPING

Use only fresh fruits, but substitute whatever is in season. You may also substitute other flavored liqueurs. Serve over banana slices, angel food cake, ice cream or frozen yogurt. Or eat it just the way it is.

2 tbs. water
1/2 tsp. cornstarch
1 tbs. orange or apricot brandy
1/2 cup sliced kiwi fruit, peeled, slices 1/4-inch thick
1/2 cup fresh blueberries
1 cup sliced fresh strawberries, slices 1/4-inch thick
1 tsp. sugar

In a small bowl, whisk together water and cornstarch. In another bowl, combine fruit with brandy and gently mix. Pour fruit mixture into a preheated nonstick skillet set over medium heat. Pour in sugar and cornstarch mixture; stir gently. Cook for 2 to 3 minutes or until sauce thickens. Remove from heat and let cool briefly before serving.

BLUEBERRY SAUCE

Serve warm or chilled over pancakes and French toast, or ice cream and frozen yogurt desserts. This recipe also makes an interesting dipping sauce for sautéed chicken.

1/4 cup water
2 tbs. honey
1/4 tsp. cinnamon
1/8 tsp. nutmeg
6 tbs. brown sugar
2 tbs. granulated sugar
2 cups blueberries, fresh or frozen

In a small 7-inch sauté pan, bring water to a boil. Quickly add honey and whisk in cinnamon, nutmeg and sugars. Add blueberries, reduce heat to medium-low, cover and simmer for 15 minutes.

BANANAS SUPREME

Servings: 4

Sautéed bananas will add a creative touch to your meal. This dessert stands alone, or try it as a topping with frozen yogurt, ice cream or cake.

3 tbs. apple juice
2 tsp. fresh lemon juice
½ tsp. cornstarch
1 tsp. granulated sugar
1 tbs. brown sugar
¼ tsp. cinnamon

⅛ tsp. nutmeg
½ tsp. vanilla extract
2 ripe bananas, peeled
1 tbs. butter
frozen yogurt, ice cream or cake, optional
2 tbs. finely choppped walnuts

In a small bowl, combine apple juice, 1 tsp. lemon juice, cornstarch, sugars, cinnamon, nutmeg and vanilla. Mix well. Cut each banana in half lengthwise, and cut each half into 2 equal lengths (4 pieces from each banana). Drizzle banana pieces with 1 tsp. of the lemon juice. Melt butter in a nonstick skillet over medium heat. Pour in apple juice mixture and heat for 2 minutes. Place banana slices in skillet and sauté for 45 seconds on each side. Serve alone or over frozen yogurt, ice cream or cake. Sprinkle with chopped walnuts. Drizzle with remaining sauce from skillet.

CINNAMON WALNUT BANANA SAUTÉ

Servings: 4

One of the best desserts is quickly made but elegant. Sift the confectioners' sugar, or place sugar in a fine mesh strainer and tap the sides.

4 bananas
juice of 1 lemon
3 tbs. butter
⅓ cup brown sugar
1 tbs. granulated sugar
⅓ tsp. cinnamon
frozen yogurt or ice cream
confectioners' sugar
⅓ cup coarsely chopped walnuts

Peel and slice bananas in half lengthwise. Cut each slice into 3- or 3½-inch pieces. Coat banana pieces with lemon juice. Melt butter in a skillet over medium-low heat. Stir in sugars and cinnamon. Sauté bananas for 1½ minutes on each side. Serve over ice cream or frozen yogurt, or serve cooked bananas on dessert plates; pour butter mixture over bananas, and top with a sprinkle of confectioners' sugar and walnuts.

SPICED APPLE WEDGES

You can serve these scrumptious appetizing treats anytime of the day. Serve warm. This recipe is always a major hit.

4 large firm apples
juice of 1 lemon
juice of 1 lime
2 cups plain breadcrumbs
1 tsp. cinnamon
⅛ tsp. nutmeg

½ tsp. grated fresh lemon rind (zest)
½ tsp. granulated sugar
2 eggs, beaten
¼ cup canola oil
confectioners' sugar

Core but do not peel apples. Slice cored apples into thin ¼-inch wedges. In a small bowl, combine lemon and lime juices. In a shallow bowl, combine breadcrumbs, cinnamon, nutmeg, lemon rind and granulated sugar. Brush apple wedges with lemon-lime juice. Coat apple wedges with egg and dredge in breadcrumb mixture. Shake off excess. Heat 2 tbs. of the oil in a skillet over medium heat. Sauté apple wedges for 2 minutes on each side or until lightly browned and cooked through. Add more oil as needed. Transfer cooked apple wedges to a paper towel-lined surface to absorb any excess oil. Place apple wedges on a serving plate and sprinkle with confectioners' sugar.

SAUTÉED APPLE RINGS

Servings: 4

You'll want to serve this simple but glorious dessert to company. For best results, use a good firm apple such as a Baldwin, Cortland, Granny Smith, Gravenstein, Golden Delicious or Rome Beauty. Serve as a side dish to pork, lamb or goose; or as a specialty dessert with frozen yogurt or vanilla ice cream.

4 large apples
juice of 1 lemon
1/2 cup butter
1/3 cup brown sugar

1/4 tsp. cinnamon
1/8 tsp. nutmeg
1/2 cup apricot or apple brandy

Peel, core and slice apples into 1/4-inch-thick rings. Coat apple rings with lemon juice. Melt 2 tbs. of the butter in a skillet over medium-high heat. Sauté apples until lightly brown, about 2 minutes on each side. Remove apples from pan and place on a warm platter. Continue to sauté all apples, adding butter as needed. When all apples have been cooked, add brown sugar, cinnamon, nutmeg and brandy. Mix thoroughly. Carefully place cooked apple rings in skillet. Cover skillet and cook over low heat for 3 to 4 minutes or until apples are hot.

VARIATION: SAUTÉED PINEAPPLE RINGS

Substitute pineapple slices for apple slices, eliminate brandy and add pineapple juice to the skillet.

SAUTÉED PEARS AMARETTI

This luscious and elegant dessert is the perfect finale for a memorable evening.

2 firm, slightly underripe pears
juice of ½ lemon
1 cup water
1 tsp. cinnamon
¼ tsp. ground cloves
¼ cup sugar
2 tbs. honey
low fat frozen yogurt
2 tbs. crumbled amaretti cookies

Peel, core and cut pears into ¼-inch-thick slices. Lightly coat pear slices with lemon juice. Pour water into a medium skillet and bring to a boil. Stir in cinnamon, cloves and sugar; reduce heat to medium. Add pear slices. Stir, cover and cook until pears are tender, about 6 minutes. Remove pears from pan and place on 2 warm serving plates. Add honey to liquid in skillet, and cook over medium heat for 5 to 8 minutes or until sauce begins to thicken and cook down. Pour sauce over pears. Top with frozen yogurt and cookie crumbles. Serve immediately.

SPICY GOLDEN PEARS

The flavor is absolutely incredible. Serve plain or over a layer of lady fingers.

2 large pears, Bartlett, Bosc or Anjou
4 cups apple juice
1 tbs. sugar
1/4 tsp. cinnamon
1/8 tsp. ground cloves
1/2 tsp. grated fresh lemon rind (zest)
1 tbs. cornstarch
whipped cream
2 tbs. chopped walnuts

Cut pears in half lengthwise. Cut out stems and remove core. Cut pear halves into 1/4-inch slices. Into a medium skillet, pour juice and bring to a boil. Stir in sugar, cinnamon, cloves and lemon rind. Add pear slices and reduce heat; simmer for 8 to 10 minutes or until tender. Remove pear slices with a slotted spoon and place on individual dessert plates. Allow liquid to remain in skillet. Slowly whisk cornstarch into liquid; continue to cook over medium-high heat, stirring frequently. After sauce reduces and thickens, pour over cooked pears. Top with whipped cream and sprinkle with chopped walnuts. Serve immediately.

HONEY PEACH SAUCE

Yield: 6 cups

Spoon peaches and sauce over ice cream, frozen yogurt, sponge cake or sliced gingerbread. It can be served hot or cold. Even people who aren't really peach fans give high raves for this dessert topping.

1 tbs. water
1 tsp. cornstarch
¾ cup applesauce
¼ cup honey
1 tbs. fresh lemon juice
⅓ tsp. cinnamon
⅛ tsp. nutmeg
5 cups fresh peach slices

In a small bowl, whisk together water and cornstarch. Pour applesauce into a small skillet over medium heat. As soon as it starts to boil, add honey, lemon juice, cinnamon and nutmeg. Simmer for 1 minute. Add peach slices and simmer for 3 to 4 minutes. Add cornstarch mixture. Stir frequently and simmer for 2 to 3 minutes. Serve warm or let cool, refrigerate and serve cold.

FRESH PINEAPPLE AND HONEY SAUTÉ

Servings: 4

This quick and beautiful pineapple sauté will stand on its own as a pleasing dessert. It's also a tasty topping to sautéed or grilled tuna or swordfish.

1 medium pineapple
2 tbs. butter
1 tbs. honey
½ tsp. chopped fresh mint
½ tsp. chopped fresh cilantro
4-6 fresh mint or cilantro leaves for garnish

Peel, core and slice pineapple into 3-inch wedges. Melt butter in a nonstick skillet over medium-low heat. Stir in honey, heat and mix well. Add pineapple, cooking all sides. Sauté for 8 minutes. Add mint and cilantro. Serve immediately on individual dessert plates. Garnish with fresh mint or cilantro leaves.

APRICOT CHERRY SAUCE

This fruit sauce adds a spectacular flair as a topping to cake and puddings.

½ cup dried apricots
½ cup dried cherries
¾ cup unsweetened pineapple juice
1 tbs. brown sugar
¼ tsp. cinnamon
⅛ tsp. allspice
½ tsp. cornstarch

Combine dried apricots, dried cherries, pineapple juice, brown sugar, cinnamon and allspice in a bowl and mix well. Pour fruit mixture into a small nonstick skillet set over medium-high heat. Bring to a boil. Reduce heat to low and simmer for 7 minutes. Stir occasionally. Lift fruit from skillet, retaining juice in skillet, and set aside. Slowly whisk cornstarch into juice. Bring to a quick boil and remove from heat. Combine sauce with fruit. Let cool before serving.

CHOCOLATE COCONUT SKILLET BAKE

Servings: 8

It's absolutely amazing to see how easy it is to make this great-tasting, bakery-quality product from a stovetop skillet. Top with ice cream, whipped cream or fresh fruit, or serve plain with fresh coffee.

⅓ cup coconut flakes
¼ cup sweetened condensed milk
⅓ cup semisweet chocolate chips
2 oz. peanut butter chips
2 egg whites

1 tbs. milk
½ tsp. vanilla extract
3 tbs. flour
¾ tsp. baking powder
⅛ tsp. salt, optional

Place coconut in a dry nonstick skillet. Toast over medium-low heat until light golden brown. Stir frequently. Remove from pan and set aside. In a 10-inch nonstick skillet, combine condensed milk, chocolate chips and peanut butter chips. Heat over low heat until chocolate is melted. In a medium bowl, whisk together egg whites, milk, vanilla, flour, baking powder and salt until well blended. Stir egg mixture into skillet with chocolate. Mix together and stir in toasted coconut flakes. Cover and cook for 15 minutes over medium-low heat. To remove from skillet, use a sharp-edged nylon spatula to release cake. Turn out in one large piece onto a plate. Cut into wedges and serve on individual dessert plates.

PINEAPPLE RIGHT-SIDE-UP CAKE

Servings: 2

We've given a new twist to an old-fashioned favorite. It's a quick and easy method to prepare dessert, yet very tasty.

1 can (8 oz.) pineapple slices with juice
2 tbs. butter
1/3 cup brown sugar
2 slices pound cake, 1 1/2-inch thick
4-6 maraschino cherries
whipped cream, optional

Remove pineapple slices from juice. Set 3 tbs. of the juice aside and refrigerate remaining juice for use in other recipes. In a small skillet, melt butter over medium heat. Whisk in brown sugar and 3 tbs. pineapple juice until well blended. Add pineapple slices and bring to a quick boil. Reduce heat to medium-low and continue to cook for 3 to 4 minutes. Place slices of pound cake on 2 individual dessert plates. Divide pineapple slices equally over pound cake and drizzle with remaining sauce from skillet. Top with cherries, and whipped cream if desired.

CARNIVAL PEANUTS

This possibly addicting snack has the essence of an old country store candy counter.

1 tbs. butter or margarine
3 tsp. maple syrup
½ tsp. granulated sugar
3 tbs. brown sugar
⅛ tsp. vanilla extract
3 cups unsalted, dry roasted peanuts
ice cream or frozen yogurt, optional

Melt butter in an 8- to 10-inch nonstick skillet over medium heat. Add maple syrup and sugars. Bring to a quick boil. Stir in vanilla. Add peanuts and stir, coating all sides. Reduce heat to medium low and cook for 5 minutes. Stir frequently. Remove from heat and let cool. Serve over ice cream of frozen yogurt if desired.

CANDY ALMONDS

Yield: 1½ cups

Kids and adults go wild over this nutty, spicy treat you can make in your skillet.

1½ cups whole almonds
1 tbs. egg whites
¼ cup sugar
1 tsp. cinnamon
⅛ tsp. nutmeg
⅛ tsp. allspice

In a large bowl, combine nuts with egg whites. In a small bowl, combine sugar and spices. Add spice mixture to nuts; mix thoroughly. Heat a large nonstick skillet over medium heat. Add nut mixture. Cook for 15 minutes, stirring frequently, or until golden brown. Let cool and transfer to a serving bowl.

INDEX